The Illustrated School Thesaurus

Introducing this Thesaurus

Imagine that you have used a word in a sentence. And you have to use the same word in the next sentence. And the next. And the next. Boring isn't it?

So instead of saying, "The pretty girl looked very pretty in her pretty dress. She went to a pretty garden where she picked some pretty flowers," it would be more interesting if we say, "The pretty girl looked very nice in her charming dress. She went to a beautiful garden where she picked some lovely flowers."

Now think of a big dinosaur in a museum. Of course, it is big, but while describing it, it would add more effect to say "I saw a huge dinosaur in the museum today," rather than "I saw a big dinosaur in the museum today."

So what you needed for the words pretty and big in the case of the examples were their synonyms. A synonym is a word which means the same or almost the same as another word. So some of the synonyms for the word pretty are nice, charming, beautiful, lovely and one of the synonyms for big is huge.

And if you want to look up the synonyms of words, you have to find them in a thesaurus, which is a collection of words and their synonyms.

In this thesaurus, the entries that have been selected are those that children between the ages of 8-12 often use or come across. Also, the synonyms that are here are those words that come closest in sense to the entry.

Apart from that, the highlight of this book is that there is a sentence for one of the synonyms of every entry to give an example of how the word may be used. Also, there are lively and witty illustrations on each page to make some of the sentences come alive and to make the journey across the thesaurus more memorable, vivid and fun.

Finding your way

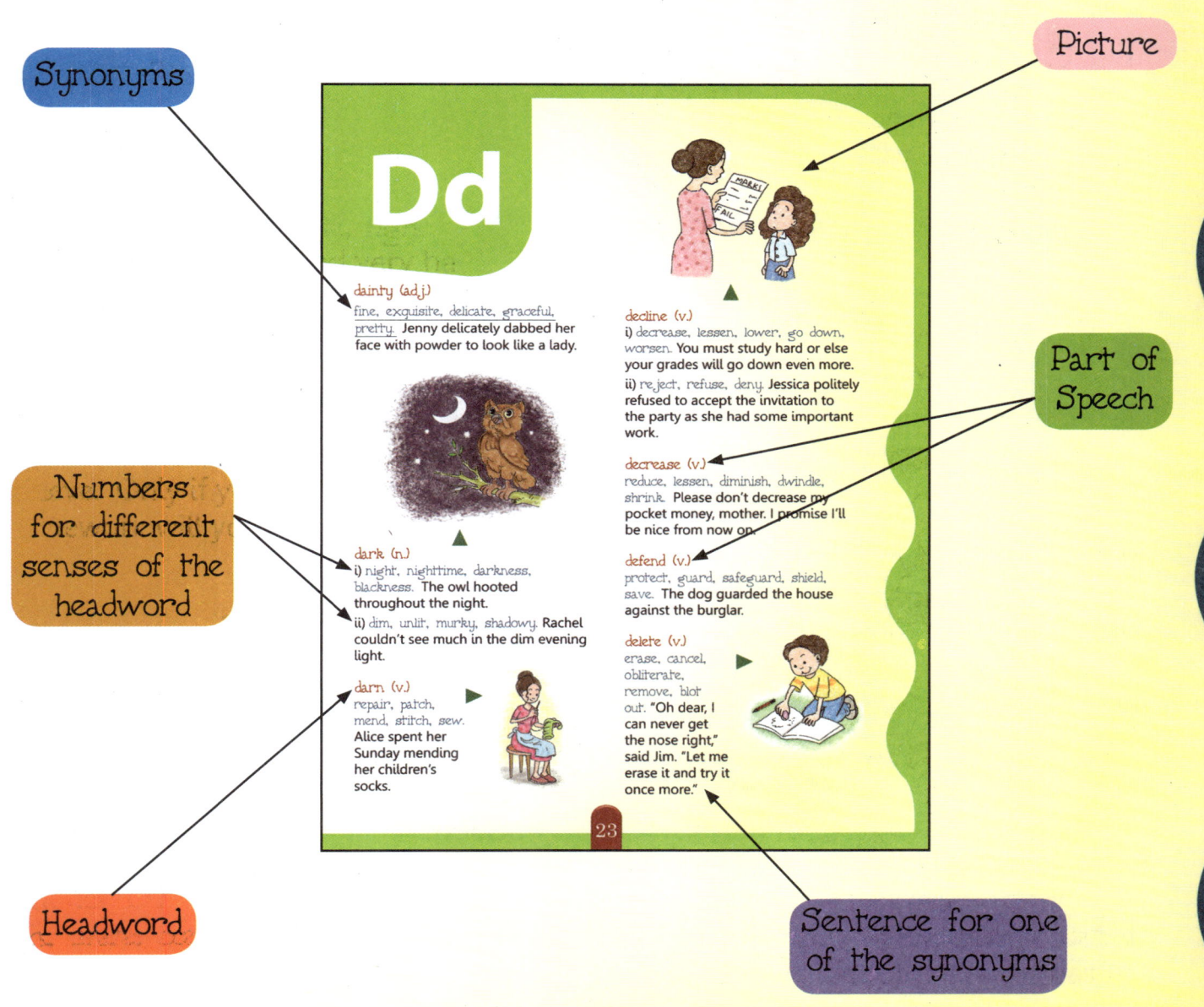

Aa

abduct (v.)
kidnap, seize, grab, snatch. Aunt Emma helped the police to identify the man who tried to kidnap little Josh.

abide (v.)
i) stay, tarry, lodge, rest, keep. You must stay here during the night because it is unsafe to travel.

ii) dwell, reside, live, inhabit, settle. The Smith family lived in a cozy cottage in the mountains.

able (adj.)
i) clever, accomplished, talented, expert, skilful. Patrick is a talented musician who can play many instruments well.

ii) capable, gifted, powerful, strong. The capable minister always gave good advice to the king.

above (prep.)
above, over, higher. The space shuttle shot up into the sky and over the clouds within a second.

abrupt (adj.)
sudden, unexpected, hasty, unannounced. The machine suddenly came to a standstill.

absurd (adj.)
unreasonable, foolish, nonsensical, ridiculous, silly, stupid. Your suggestion that I go home in this heavy rain is ridiculous.

abundant (adj.)
abounding, overflowing, plentiful, bountiful, rich. This winter, we had a bountiful harvest of wheat and rice.

accept (v.)
i) take, receive, obtain, acquire, have. Frank was happy to take the award from his headmistress.

ii) admit, agree to, approve, embrace, acknowledge. Pam was admitted into medical school because she was a bright student.

accident (n.)
casualty, misadventure, calamity, mishap, misfortune. A mishap occurred as soon as Martha lost control of the car.

accomplish (v.)
complete, achieve, perform, do, carry out, finish. The Wright brothers achieved their task of building a flying machine.

accumulate (v.)
pile, amass, collect, collect together, heap. Henry had collected the rarest coins for his coin collection.

accurate (adj.)
exact, correct, precise, true, faithful. Please respond correctly to all the questions I ask you.

achieve (v.)
i) accomplish, perform, finish, work out. The mountaineer accomplished his dream when he climbed the highest peak in the world.

ii) obtain, acquire, procure, gain, win, get. The prince finally won the hand of the princess he loved.

acknowledge (v.)
i) recognise, be aware of. William's efforts were finally recognised and he was awarded.

ii) admit, grant, concede, allow, accept, agree to. Hank admitted that he had made a mistake.

acquaint (v.)
i) familiarize, make familiar. "Please familiarize yourself with the safety instructions," announced the air hostess.

ii) inform, tell, notify, mention to, communicate to. The detective was not informed about how the theft had taken place.

action (n.)
i) activity, work, effort, deed, doing, performance, feat, exploit. Larry liked to read about the deeds of heroes.

ii) battle, conflict, combat, encounter, skirmish. This memorial is dedicated to soldiers killed in battle in the Second World War.

active (adj.)
i) functioning, working, operating. This machine is in an operating condition even after many years.

ii) busy, bustling, diligent, industrious. Everyone hurriedly walked along the busy street.

iii) alert, agile, brisk, lively, spirited, energetic. Old Roger was so energetic that he could run faster than a lot of young men.

actual (adj.)
real, true, objective, certain, genuine. This is a story based on real facts.

acute (adj.)
i) sharp, pointed. The soldier was proud of the pointed tip of his sword.

ii) keen, shrewd, knowing, quick, sharp, smart, bright. Tracy has a keen sense of smell.

iii) severe, intense, distressing, fierce, piercing. While clearing the table, mother suddenly groaned and complained of severe pain in her back.

adapt (v.)
adjust, accommodate, suit, fit, conform. It was difficult for Greg to adjust to a new school in a new town.

add (v.)
i) join, tag, tack on, connect, attach. "Let's join the beds together for tonight. We have so much to talk about," said Janice to her cousin, Maureen.

ii) sum, sum up, total, add together, aggregate. Quickly sum up the number of plates and spoons we have before the guests arrive.

adjust (v.)

i) arrange, rectify, trim, order. "Arrange the room before mom comes and scolds you," said Daisy to her sister Lucy.

ii) fit, adapt, suit, accommodate, measure. This suit has to be fitted because it is too large for you.

admire (v.)
esteem, regard, honour, think highly of, prize, value. I esteem those who act bravely.

adorn (v.)
embellish, decorate, beautify, ornament, set, grace. Tina decorated the entrance to her house with holly, mistletoe and colourful lights for Christmas.

adult (adj.)
mature, grown up, of age, of mature age. Peter Pan never wanted to act like a grown up.

advance (v.)
i) propose, offer, bring forward, lay down. Alec offered his suggestion that we practise for two hours and then go for lunch.

ii) proceed, progress, go forward, rise, march. The army progressed steadily towards the enemy.

adversary (n.)
enemy, foe, antagonist, opponent. Be ready or else your opponent will strike when you're not looking.

advice (n.)
counsel, suggestion, instruction, recommendation, warning, caution. Dad's recommendation to Ken was to practise more so that he could get his timing right.

afraid (adj.)
fearful, frightened, terrified, scared, timid. The whole town was fearful when they saw the monster.

agree (v.)
i) accept, consent, assent. Jim finally accepted my idea to go to the amusement park.

ii) correspond, coincide, fit, match. What John said did not match with what Peter had said.

aim (v.)
i) direct, level, point, train. William pointed the tip of the arrow carefully towards the target and shot.

(n.)
ii) intent, purpose, scheme, reason, goal, point. Barry's goal in life was to become an astronaut.

alike (adj.)
similar, like, resembling, identical, twin. Gabriella and her mom look very similar.

allure (v.)
entice, tempt, lure, invite, attract. The evil witch enticed Hansel and Gretel with a house made of sweets and trapped them.

alone (adj.)
single, solitary, sole, lone, lonely. The prisoner was held in solitary confinement.

alter (adj.)
change, vary, modify, deviate. "You have to change your attitude and not throw tantrums like this," said mother to Molly.

always (adv.)
constantly, ever after, forever, continually, repeatedly. "I will remember this forever," Sam said when he got a surprise party on his birthday.

amaze (v.)
astonish, astound, surprise, daze, stupefy. Everyone was astonished when they saw the rabbit disappear into the magician's hat.

ancient (adj.)
old, aged, primitive, antique, old-fashioned. The wealthy merchant bought antique clocks and sold them at a very high price.

anecdote (n.)
tale, story, yarn, sketch. Gina loved telling stories about interesting incidents in her life to everyone.

anger (v.)
irritate, displease, provoke, enrage, madden, make angry. When the dog attacked Freddie, he was provoked to throw stones at it.

answer (v..)
reply, rejoin, respond, retort. "Are we there yet?" Andy asked dad. "No, we're still a long way off," he replied.

ape (v.)
mimic, imitate, copy. "Stop aping me!" Sarah told her brother when he was copying all that she said and did.

appear (v.)
i) emerge, come in sight, be visible, loom, show itself, turn up. We took flight when a crocodile emerged from the lake all of a sudden.

ii) seem, look, show. It seemed to Ali that there was an oasis in front of him but there wasn't.

arid (adj.)
dry, dried up, parched, infertile, barren. The new well was beneficial to all the villagers in the dry region.

around (adv.)
on every side, about, surrounding, enclosing. There was a stillness in the air surrounding the manor on top of the hill.

arrive (v.)
reach, turn up, come, enter, get to. Jake looked at the train entering the station.

assist (v.)
help, aid, support, serve, back, cooperate. Stanley aided the police at catching the thief.

attend (v.)
i) guard, watch, protect, have in keeping. Benji guards the garden from stray cats.

ii) appear, be present, frequent, visit, turn up. You must be present at the school function tomorrow.

(v.)
listen, hear, give ear, give heed, pay attention. "Now listen carefully boys," said Miss Jane. "Today I shall educate you about the human skeletal system."

attract (v.)
allure, pull, entice, fascinate, charm. The shine of the gold allured the greedy man towards it and he stole all of it.

authentic (adj.)
i) genuine, real, true, pure, uncorrupted. This document certifies that the gold that has been given to you is genuine.

ii) trustworthy, reliable, true, accurate. The Bennet family left the house in the care of their reliable neighbour, Mr. Willis when they went on holiday.

awake (v.)
arise, rouse, wake, stir. It was already afternoon when Susan arose from sleep.

awful (adj.)
terrible, foul, dreadful, horrible, bad. Lisa looked at the heavy rain outside her window and said, "Oh my! what terrible weather!"

awkward (adj.)
unskilful, bungling, blundering, clumsy. What a pair of bungling kids Ted and Harry are! Wherever they go, there's always something breaking or falling.

Bb

back (n.)
i) behind, rear, reverse. Watch out Tim, you will damage all the pretty flowers behind you.
(v.)
ii) support, favour, encourage. Pat's parents supported his decision to go to art school.

bad (adj.)
i) evil, ill, harmful, hurtful, injurious. The evil witch planned to eat up the children.
ii) foul, decayed, rotten, spoiled, polluted. The food has become spoiled and there are flies on it.

baffle (v.)
confuse, puzzle, perplex, bewilder. "Numbers always confuse me," thought Peter.

banish (v.)
expel, exile, deport, outlaw. The wicked prince was exiled by the king because he oppressed the villagers.

battle (n.)
combat, action, conflict, contest, fight. The officer commanded the troops to be ready for combat.
(v.)
contend with, struggle, strive for, do battle, fight. The two teams fought hard to win the trophy.

beacon (n.)
light, signal, beam, guide, lighthouse. The lighthouse flashed its light to lost sailors at sea.

beam (n.)
i) girder, support, rafter, timber. I felt really unsafe standing under the crumbling rafters of the old shack, fearing that the roof might cave in anytime.
ii) ray, streak, flash, stream, shaft. While rowing his boat towards the island, Matt saw a ray of light flashing towards him from the shore.

beast (n.)
i) animal, creature, mammal. A huge creature appeared in front of George and he was scared stiff.
ii) savage, ogre, brute, monster. The glowing eyes of the monster looked eerie in the dark.

bedraggled (adj.)
messy, dirty, disordered, untidy, unkempt. Even though his hair was unkempt, the movie star looked dashing.

before (adv.)
back, earlier, previously. Every morning, Tim woke up earlier than his brother.

beg (v.)
implore, pray, plead, request, ask. Joan pleaded with her father to get the grey dog but he insisted on getting the brown one.

begin (v.)
originate, arise, start, emerge, appear. Most rivers arise when the snow melts in the mountains.

beautiful (adj.)
gorgeous, appealing, lovely, pretty, attractive. Tanya stood in the lovely garden and took a very deep breath.

bend (v.)
bow, curve, turn, twist, stoop. Norman is so strong that he can curve an iron rod with his bare hands.

big (adj.)
large, great, immense, enormous, gigantic, massive. Timmy felt like a puny elf sitting on the large elephant.

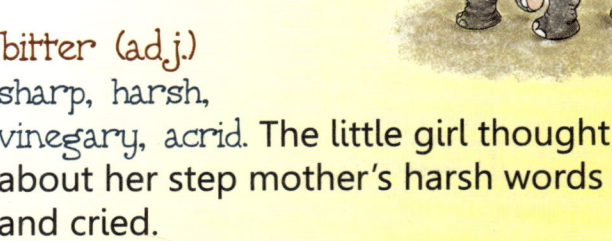

bitter (adj.)
sharp, harsh, vinegary, acrid. The little girl thought about her step mother's harsh words and cried.

blank (adj.)
i) empty, plain, white, clear, bare. Penelope took out a plain sheet of paper and began to write an exquisite poem.

ii) puzzled, muddled, confused, bewildered. Jerry spoke so fast that everyone around him had puzzled expressions on their faces.

bloat (v.)
swell, inflate, puff up, blow up. We inflated the boat and went rafting on it.

block (v.)
obstruct, clog, stop, choke, jam, hinder. The clogged sink overflowed and messed up the bathroom floor.

blossom (v.)
flower, bloom, grow, mature, flourish. Flowers wither and fall in the autumn only to bloom again in spring.

blow (v.)
i) thump, swipe, stroke, knock. The strong woodcutter cut the tree with only five strokes of his axe.

ii) blast, puff, breathe, exhale. The wolf huffed and puffed and he blew the house down.

blunder (n.)
mistake, error, lapse, slip. Homer performed the role of a pirate king without making even a single mistake.

bold (adj.)
i) fearless, daring, spirited, audacious, courageous, brave. Alice is a courageous girl. She dived into the water to save Anna.

ii) confident, assured. Heather acted confidently on stage and spoke her lines with ease.

book (n.)
paperback, novel, text, volume, manuscript. The old professor had huge volumes stacked up in his library.

(v.)
reserve, arrange for, make reservations. Father called up and reserved a table for us at the restaurant.

boon (n.)
blessing, grant, benefit, gift, present. After a parched summer, the rain came as a blessing to the farmers.

bother (v.)
worry, trouble, annoy, disturb, pester, irritate. Don't trouble me Johnny. Can't you see that I am reading?

brave (adj.)
fearless, daring, gallant, courageous, bold. The gallant prince rescued the princess from the fiery dragon.

brawl (v.)
quarrel, dispute, wrangle, squabble, bicker. A loud quarrel broke out in the street when grandpa's car blocked the road.

brawny (adj.)
muscular, strong, athletic, able-bodied. The muscular man lifted the motorcycle very easily.

break (v.)
i) crack, fracture, wreck, smash. Although he is quite old, grandfather can still crack walnuts with his teeth.

ii) exceed, beat, top. The runner beat the world record for the fastest timing in the 100 metres race.

bright (adj.)
i) shining, sparkling, dazzling, illuminated. The shining lamp lit up the dark, rainy evening.

ii) clever, smart, intelligent, quick. What a smart girl! She answered all the questions.

bring (v.)
i) bear, fetch, get, carry, take. Billy, will you hurry? You are taking so long to fetch the water!

ii) produce, effect, create, cause, result in. The rains in the middle of the hot summer resulted in cool weather.

brisk (adj.)
energetic, lively, quick, vigorous, active. "We will reach the bus stop on time only if we walk quickly," said Wayne to his sister.

bruise (n.)
mark, injury, blemish, swelling. Davy, I can't bandage your injury if you wriggle your toes.

(v.)
injure, hurt, wound, insult, pain. Joshua fell from the cycle and wounded himself.

buffoon (n.)
joker, clown, fool, jester. Look at the clown in the hula hoop circling the ring.

build (v.)
construct, make, create, manufacture. "Daddy, can you please make a doll's house for me?" asked Nora.

bunch (n.)
cluster, clump, bundle, group, heap. The worker tied up the bundles of hay and kept them ready for the sale.

burn (v.)
ignite, singe, scorch, light, blaze. We all gathered round the fireplace where the fire blazed away and we felt very cosy.

bush (n.)
shrub, thicket, hedge, shrubbery. Louisa looked all around for her cat which was actually hiding in the thicket.

buy (v.)
purchase, take, acquire, obtain, get. Purchase three bags and get a shirt free!

by (prep.)
close to, next to, beside, near, alongside. Harriet parked her car near the water hydrant and walked to the coffee shop.

(adv.)
next to, close to, along, past, near. Everyone waved at the soldiers when they marched past them.

Cc

cab (n.)
taxi, cabriolet, taxicab. Fleming hailed a taxi to return home.

cabin (n.)
cottage, hut, lodge, shack. Below the blue mountains is a small cosy cottage.

cackle (v.)
i) chuckle, laugh, giggle, titter, snicker. Uncle Billy chuckled heartily at Philip's jokes at the family dinner.

ii) chatter, prattle, babble. "Don't chatter while you eat, or else you'll choke," mother scolded Dora.

call (v.)
i) shout, yell, cry, hail. "Ma, have you seen my blue pen," cried out Penny from her room.

ii) invite, ask, bid, summon. I'll invite Betty and Frank to my birthday too.

iii) phone, telephone, dial, ring. "You can ring me up any time you need help," told the teacher to Jerry.

calm (adj.)
still, quiet, peaceful, serene, undisturbed. The boat sailed on the still waters of the lake.

capacity (n.)
i) size, dimensions, scope, volume, room, space. There is no room in this small place for both of us.

ii) ability, capability, skill, potential, aptitude. I have practised this game to the best of my ability.

captain (n.)
commander, leader, chief, skipper, pilot. The commander of the ship took very good care of the crew and everyone was fond of him.

captivate (v.)
charm, fascinate, enchant, enthrall, bewitch, enamour. Adventure and detective stories never failed to fascinate Nathan.

17

care (v.)

i) protect, attend, watch, tend. "Tend the sheep carefully," said the older shepherd to the new one.

ii) like, wish, want, desire. Would you like another cup of tea?

iii) worry, concern, burden, responsibility. The little boy was happy playing football and didn't have anything to worry about in the whole wide world.

iv) caution, attention, watchfulness. Mrs. Brett contioned the children not to play by the pool as it was deep.

carry (v.)

bear, bring, move, haul, lug. Gary found it difficult to bear the heavy load.

carton (n.)

box, container, case, package, crate. I packed all my books in a box and put it in the boot of the car.

case (n.)

i) example, event, circumstance, state, occasion, situation. In the event of an emergency, give me a call.

ii) cover, envelope, folder, wrapper, sheath. Please put the letter in the envelope before sending it.

catch (v.)

i) grab, grasp, seize, snatch, grasp. Marie grabbed hold of Teresa's hand when she was about to fall off the ladder.

ii) arrest, capture. The policeman captured the runaway prisoner and brought him back to prison.

iii) ensnare, entrap, entangle, net. The poor bird was entangled in the birdcatcher's nest.

caution (n.)

alertness, care, watchfulness, heed. Take care when you are standing on the roof. It has no railing.

cheer (v.)

i) encourage, buck up, applaud. "Candice, you should never give up your hobby of painting," encouraged mother.

ii) console, comfort, brighten, reassure. Keith cracked jokes to brighten up Lily when she was sad.

chew (v.)
chomp, bite, munch, gnaw, crunch. Grandfather hungrily chomped through the apple.

chill (n.)
coolness, coldness, frostiness, nip. There's a nip in the air and so I'll have to wear a muffler.

(adj.)
icy, cold, cool, frosty. We finally escaped the hot summer and went to the mountains where it was icy and cold.

(v.)
cool, refrigerate, freeze, frost. You have to cool this drink before you serve it.

choose (v.)
select, pick, take, elect, adopt. Mother picked wholesome cereals for the children's breakfast from the supermarket.

clean (v.)
wash, bathe, cleanse, wipe, sweep, neaten. Grace helped her father wash the car every saturday morning.

(adj.)
i) washed, spotless, fresh, flawless. To sleep on fresh bedsheets is always a delight.

ii) healthy, pure, unpolluted, uncontaminated. The unpolluted air of the hills is refreshing to the soul.

clear (adj.)
i) transparent, colourless, see-through. I can see you hiding behind the transparent curtain, Jeff.

ii) unobstructed, free, open, empty, smooth. It's delightful to drive down the open road with the breeze blowing your hair.

iii) serene, fair, cloudless, sunny. A cool sunny day and cloudless skies made it a perfect day for an outing.

(v.)
i) free, empty, remove, open, unblock. Finally, the clogged drains were opened after the plumber arrived.

ii) sweep, scour, clean up. There are toys all around the room. Do clean it up.

clever (adj.)
skilful, ingenious, quick, smart, intelligent. Besides being intelligent, Beth was diligent with her work.

climb (v.)
go up, mount, soar, rise, ascend, scale. The rocket quickly ascended into the skies.

close (v.)
i) shut, lock, seal. On Sundays, all the shops are shut.

ii) finish, end, conclude, cease. The principal concluded the term by wishing everyone, "Happy holidays".

clumsy (adj.)
awkward, bungling, blundering, unskillful. Stanley is such a bungling person that he keeps dropping things all the time.

coarse (adj.)
rough, irregular, uneven. Years of hard work in the mines had made Vincent's hands very rough.

collect (v.)
gather, assemble, accumulate, compile. Since I am going to visit grandmother, I shall gather some flowers for her.

comical (adj.)
humorous, funny, laughable, amusing. You should have seen the way they wore their hats. It was so laughable.

comfortable (adj.)
i) agreeable, cozy, snug, pleasant, pleasing, soft. Lily hugged her snug toy bear.

ii) relaxed, at ease, restful, calm, contented, happy. Harold felt very relaxed lying down to rest after a hard day's work.

common (adj.)
commonplace, regular, familiar, ordinary, usual. Hank was tired of his hometown because it had become too familiar to him. That is why he wanted to travel.

compassion (n.)
pity, sympathy, tenderness, kindness, mercy. Uncle Tom showed kindness to the ragamuffin girl by giving her warm clothes during winter.

compete (v.)
contend, strive, struggle, fight, challenge. Mark practised very hard so that he could contend for the gold medal in the school race.

complete (v.)
i) finish, end, conclude, accomplish, achieve. Only if you finish your homework will you be allowed to play.

ii) total, whole, entire, full. You must eat the whole apple.

conceal (v.)
hide, cover, mask, bury, cover up, disguise. Pinocchio covered up his lies by telling even more lies.

connect (v.)
join, unite, combine, associate, link. The 7th Avenue is linked to Park Street by a flyover.

conquer (v.)
vanquish, subdue, defeat, overthrow, beat. It was not easy for the Greeks to defeat the brave Trojans.

continue (v.)
i) remain, last, endure, stay, keep up, maintain. The snow is very beautiful but it will not last when the sun comes out.

ii) extend, lengthen, prolong, draw out, proceed. Kirk extended his stay in Paris by two more days.

correct (adj.)
faultless, exact, precise, accurate, right, true. "This answer is right," said the teacher to Dave.

costly (adj.)
expensive, pricey, steep, high-priced. The jewellery I saw at the shop was very expensive.

cover (v.)
i) coat, envelop, wrap, spread. Mother spread the cheese on the bread and called the children for breakfast.
ii) shield, protect, defended, guard. The house protected the people inside from the raging storm.

(n.)
lid, cap, top. Can you please put the lid on this box of sweets? There are too many flies in here.

crazy (adj.)
insane, mad, lunatic, deranged, cracked, crazed. "The kids run around and shout so much that they drive me insane," the babysitter told mom.

crooked (adj.)
twisted, irregular, bent, curved. "How uneven and irregular this road is!" thought Alice.

crude (adj.)
coarse, primate, unpolished, rude, clumsy. The town mouse was embarrassed by the country mouse because he thought that he was coarse.

cruel (adj.)
savage, merciless, heartless, ruthless. The heartless king took away all the land from the farmers.

cry (v.)
i) sob, lament, bawl, wail, weep. "Oh no!" sobbed Daisy. "I've dropped my ice cream."
ii) scream, shriek, screech, howl, yell, roar. "Chris, obey your elders," mother screamed angrily.

cultivate (v.)
till, plough, work, tend, prepare. Luke was busy ploughing the field the whole of last week.

cunning (adj.)
crafty, sly, wily, shrewd, crooked. The poor villager fell prey to the crafty money lender's evil plans.

curl (v.)
curve, loop, twine, coil, twirl, twist. Jackie stood in front of the mirror for hours, trying to twist her hair, hoping that it would curl.

Dd

dainty (adj.)
fine, exquisite, delicate, graceful, pretty. Jenny delicately dabbed her face with powder to look like a lady.

dark (n.)
i) night, nighttime, darkness, blackness. The owl hooted throughout the night.

ii) dim, unlit, murky, shadowy. Rachel couldn't see much in the dim evening light.

darn (v.)
repair, patch, mend, stitch, sew. Alice spent her Sunday mending her children's socks.

decline (v.)
i) decrease, lessen, lower, go down, worsen. You must study hard or else your grades will go down even more.

ii) reject, refuse, deny. Jessica politely refused to accept the invitation to the party as she had some important work.

decrease (v.)
reduce, lessen, diminish, dwindle, shrink. Please don't decrease my pocket money, mother. I promise I'll be nice from now on.

defend (v.)
protect, guard, safeguard, shield, save. The dog guarded the house from burglars.

delete (v.)
erase, cancel, obliterate, remove, blot out. "Oh dear, I can never get the nose right," said Jim. "Let me erase it and try it once more."

delicate (adj.)
i) fine, dainty, exquisite, elegant, graceful. Cathy daintily bowed to the audience after her dance.

ii) frail, fragile, slight, flimsy. The butterflies flapped their frail wings as they flit from flower to flower.

delight (n.)
joy, gladness, satisfaction, gratification, ecstasy. Frederick jumped with joy after he scored his first goal.

deserted (adj.)
forsaken, abandoned, given up, cast off, lonely. We arrived at a very lonely area at night and were scared.

destroy (v.)
ruin, wreck, demolish, level, pull down, raze. If you ruin my sandcastle, I'll go and tell mom.

develop (v.)
evolve, unfold, grow, progress, ripen, mature. The ugly duckling evolved into a beautiful swan.

different (adj.)
separate, distinct, varied, dissimilar, unlike. The Drew twins are very dissimilar in their habits.

difficult (adj.)
hard, arduous, tough, painful. The exam was very tough. The sums were too hard for me to solve.

devil (n.)
fiend, imp, satan, evildoer. The fiendish dog bit everyone he saw.

disaster (n.)
mishap, misfortune, calamity, catastrophe, blow. A lot of people died in the mishap when the bus toppled over the bridge.

disguise (v.)
conceal, cloak, veil, shroud, mask, hide. Aaron did not want anyone to recognize him at the fair, so he concealed himself by wearing a wig and dark glasses.

(n.)
mask, cover, concealment, veil. Travis wore a mask to scare everyone at the party.

dishonest (adj.)
faithless, false, deceitful, treacherous, crooked, slippery. The deceitful thug tricks people out of their money by lying to them.

dismiss (v.)
discharge, send away, discard, turn out, send packing. The prince sent away his servant because he kept making mistakes.

display (v.)
exhibit, show, reveal, expose, unveil. Dora's paintings were exhibited in the gallery.

(n.)
exhibition, exhibit, presentation, show. The puppet show left the children delighted at the end.

disturb (v.)
interrupt, annoy, trouble, bother, pester. The loud firecrackers bothered little Jeremy a lot.

doubtful (adj.)
i) unclear, vague, indefinite, questionable, unlikely. It was unclear as to how long Ben and Denise would have to wait for the train to come.

ii) uncertain, unsure, wavering, undecided, perplexed. Maurice was unsure if it was safe to walk in the dark alley.

doze (v.)
snooze, wink, siesta, nap, slumber. Fred was so lazy that he snoozed whenever he got the chance to.

drab (adj.)
dull, dreary, gloomy, shabby, dingy. Renee painted the old drab fence to make it look new.

draft (n.)
outline, sketch, plan, synopsis, rough. The writer prepared an outline of the story he was about to write.

drench (v.)
soak, wet, immerse, flood. Grandpa got soaked in the rain despite his umbrella.

drift (v.)
cruise, glide, hover, sail, waft. Thomas enjoyed the beautiful sight, while gliding over the rocky cliffs.

drowsy (adj.)
sleepy, lethargic, tired, nodding, heavy. Mr. Wilson suddenly felt very tired and sleepy and wanted to go home immediately.

dull (adj.)
i) dreary, flat, colourless, plain, uninteresting. Everyone was yawning because the speech was really uninteresting.

ii) dim-witted, stupid, unintelligent, slow, thick. Don't think I'm stupid Charlie. I know you're hiding the book behind your back.

Ee

eager (adj.)
avid, enthusiastic, excited, willing. Tom was excited when he described his New York trip to Sally.

earn (v.)
get, gain, receive, make, draw. "Here you go, Tommy," said the boss, "This is the bonus you get for working hard."

earnest (adj.)
sincere, serious, intent, determined, firm. "Your sincere effort has won you this prize and I'm proud of you," said the father praising his son.

easy (adj.)
simple, effortless, painless, light. Doing the dishes and making coffee was an effortless task for Jim.

eat (v.)
swallow, gobble, munch, chew, devour. Gary was so hungry that he devoured a whole bowl of spaghetti in five minutes.

ecstasy (n.)
joy, bliss, elation, rapture, delight. It is sheer bliss to have two wonderful daughters who are like angels.

edge (n.)
border, boundary, margin. Don't write on the margins of the book.

edible (adj.)
eatable, harmless, good, wholesome, palatable, fit to eat. Some mushrooms are fit to be eaten, but others are poisonous.

eerie (adj.)
spooky, scary, weird, mysterious, ghostly. The fog shrouded the spooky marshes and we walked cautiously through them.

efficient (adj.)
effective, able, well-organized, competent, productive. "This vacuum cleaner is so effective," thought mother.

effort (n.)
attempt, try, pains, struggle, toil. Derek took great pains to climb up the rope to his tree house.

elaborate (adj.)
detailed, complex, complicated, fancy, decorated. Poor little Kelly found herself in a very complicated maze. It took her hours to find her way out.

(v.)
explain, clarify, expand, develop. The person at the museum explained to us how humans had descended from the apes.

elder (n.)
senior, older, first-born. Elsa plays hopscotch every afternoon along with her older sister Fiona.

elegant (adj.)
graceful, majestic, grand, stylish, refined, polished. The princess was a graceful dancer.

eliminate (v.)
erase, remove, drop, eradicate, throw out. The Mayor of Hamelin pleaded with the Pied Piper to eradicate the rats that were tormenting the town.

elongate (v.)
stretch, lengthen, prolong, extend, draw out. I'll just try to lengthen these small strings by tying one to the other.

embark (v.)
i) board, sail, leave, depart. Sinbad set sail for another one of his exciting adventures in faraway lands.

ii) start, begin, launch, undertake. Once you've started this work, do not give up until you've finished it.

embarrass (v.)
fluster, humiliate, shame, upset, distress. Chuck was flustered when Sandra kissed him on his cheek in front of everyone to wish him 'Happy Birthday'.

embrace (v.)
hug, hold, caress, clasp. Sandra hugged her puppy when she got back home.

emotion (n.)
passion, feeling, fervour, sentiment, excitement. The father bade farewell with great feeling to his daughter who was going away to another country.

empire (n.)
dominion, rule, kingdom, realm, territory. At the beach, Luke built his kingdom of sandcastles.

empty (adj.)
vacant, bare, unoccupied. The old mansion was vacant and it was scary inside. But Heather and Joan were brave enough to go in and explore it.

enchant (v.)
captivate, fascinate, charm, bewitch. The prince was so bewitched by the beauty of the princess that when he saw her, he walked straight into a tree.

encourage (v.)
hearten, inspire, support, urge, strengthen. Tales of bravery and courage inspired Patrick to be brave in his own life.

end (v.)
finish, stop, conclude, halt, close, cease. The stormy winds ceased to blow, so the pioneers proceeded on their journey to find new and distant lands.

(n.)
i) finish, conclusion, close, completion. The trip was exciting from the beginning to the end.

ii) limit, boundary, border, edge, tip. "Move away from the edge of the mountain before you fall!" shouted Aunt Peggy.

enemy (n.)
foe, opponent, adversary, rival. Sam and Terry were bitter foes. But they finally made peace and later became the best of friends.

energy (n.)
might, force, strength, vigour, power. Ron pushed little Polly with all his might.

enjoy (v.)
delight, relish, like, love, savour, fancy, adore. How I relish strawberry ice cream! Of course, when I have it I'm not going to share it with you.

enlarge (v.)
inflate, magnify, stretch, expand, increase. Joey blew into the balloon and watched it expand.

enormous (adj.)
huge, massive, giant, gigantic, immense, colossal. Look at that massive elephant!

enter (v.)
come, arrive, go into, pass into, penetrate. The thief got into the room through the window while Bob was sleeping soundly.

entire (adj.)
complete, whole, full, total. "I will have my full pizza, not a slice of it," said hungry Allan.

entrance (n.)
door, doorway, gate, gateway, entry. The children became very excited the moment they passed through the gateway of the amusement park.

error (n.)
mistake, flaw, fault, slip, oversight. "There seems to be some design flaw in this T.V. set," muttered Jerry. But the truth was that it was just unplugged.

escape (v.)
i) flee, fly, get away, slip away, break out. An alarm was raised when two convicts broke out of prison.

ii) avoid, dodge, duck, evade. Katie avoided being hit by a speeding car by jumping to her right.

even (adj.)
plane, smooth, level, flat, uniform. Gilda skated gracefully on the smooth ice.

evident (adj.)
obvious, clear, plain, visible, noticeable. It was obvious to everyone that Moriarty was the murderer.

exact (adj.)
right, precise, accurate, correct, faultless. The tailor took precise measurements to make a suit for Danny.

29

examine (v.)
inspect, check, investigate, research, scan, study. The headmaster was busy inspecting the children's uniforms.

excavate (v.)
dig, unearth, shovel, scoop, uncover. The archeologists unearthed a rare gem.

excel (v.)
outdo, better, outshine, exceed, beat. Coco was such a smart dog that he outdid all the others to win first prize at the dog show.

excellent (adj.)
fantastic, fine, outstanding, superb, great, wonderful. "What a superb meal, I must say!" said Daphne to her friend, "I'm full and I'm satisfied."

excess (adj.)
extra, spare, surplus, remaining, overflow. There was a lot of extra food left over after the party.

exclaim (v.)
cry, utter, shout, yell, call. "Oh look!" cried Polly, "The mango seed has sprouted!"

exhaust (v.)
tire, weaken, fatigue, drain, wear out. "I'm so tired after running so much," Charlie told Billy as he huffed.

exit (v.)
i) depart, go, retreat, leave, withdraw. Cinderella departed from the royal ball in a hurry as she was getting very late.

ii) gate, door, way out, outlet. "The exit to the theatre is on the right," said the usher.

expand (v.)
enlarge, swell up, increase, stretch. The school office asked me to enlarge my photograph for the ID.

explain (v.)
clarify, elaborate, teach, describe, define. Josh explained to his mother that he hadn't broken the glass.

explode (v.)
burst, blow, erupt. Frank burst a balloon and scared the timid cat away.

extend (v.)
stretch, elongate, lengthen, increase. Pam stretched the rubber band so much that it broke.

Ff

fact (n.)
reality, actuality, truth. These things actually happened.

fade (v.)
dim, dull, weaken, pale, discolour. The lights dimmed before the starting of the play.

fable (n.)
i) story tale, parable, allegory, myth, legend. The teacher told us to act out the story of the lion and the rabbit.

ii) falsehood, lie, untruth, invention, fabrication, figment. "Stop telling me those lies about why you were late to class," the teacher told Brett.

fair (adj.)
just, impartial, unbiased, unprejudiced. The kingdom prospered and everyone was happy when it was ruled by a wise and just ruler.

faith (n.)
believe, trust, confidence. Mark could not trust the rope to support him any more. It was wearing out.

fake (n.)
phony, bogus, false, unreal. The guy digging a hole in the yard looked phony.

(v.)
pretend, feign, counterfeit. "No mummy," said Ron. "I'm not pretending. I really do have a stomach ache and I can't go to school."

fall (v.)
tumble, slip, plunge, crash. Danny was happily walking along the road when he suddenly tumbled into a ditch.

false (adj.)
i) incorrect, wrong, faulty, mistaken, untrue, inaccurate. The report that the murderer had been discovered was untrue.

ii) artificial, fake, bogus, mock, sham. The spy always gave everyone a fake name whereas his real name was Mr. G. Hardy.

falter (v.)
waver, hesitate, fluctuate, shake, stumble. Gayle's steps faltered as he grew more tired.

famous (adj.)
well-known, renowned, popular, eminent. Mrs. Smith's Bakery is well-known for its delicious pastries.

fast (adj.)
swift, rapid, quick, speedy. Kathy thought she was being followed by a ghost so she took rapid strides through the dark courtyard.

fasten (v.)
secure, bind, tie, attach, fix, chain. The mountain climber tied himself tight so there was no way he could fall.

fat (adj.)
i) chubby, obese, stout, plump. Toby is a chubby boy. Everyone loves to pull his cheeks, but he doesn't like it.

ii) thick, broad, large. "Oh my, what a thick book you have there!" said Tessa to Jerry.

fault (n.)
i) flaw, defect, deficiency, blemish, lack. There was not a single flaw in Celine's voice when she sang.

ii) error, mistake, blunder, guilt, responsibility. Candy had to revise her book report because there were lots of mistakes in it.

favourite (adj.)
dear, darling, beloved, precious, loved. Mother cuddled her precious baby and put him to sleep.

fear (n.)
terror, phobia, fright, dread, horror. The giant monster struck terror into the hearts of all those who saw it.

fearless (adj.)
brave, courageous, bold, valiant. The brave prince rescued the princess from the fiery dragon.

feast (n.)
celebration, banquet, dinner, meal. The king called all his knights to the grand banquet to celebrate the victory.

feeble (adj.)
infirm, weak, sickly, frail, powerless. Hugh turned weak in his knees when the lion roared at him.

ferocious (adj.)
fierce, vicious, savage, violent, cruel. Though this giant looks fierce, he is actually very gentle.

fetch (v.)
retrieve, bring, get, obtain, grab. Freddie threw a stick and the dog retrieved it for him.

fight (v.)
quarrel, battle, struggle, contend. The pirates battled strong winds and heavy rain at sea.

fill (v.)
i) stuff, cram, pack, store, load, jam. Angelina crammed the jar with chocolates and smiled a big smile.

ii) refill, supply, provide, charge. Jack charged himself with as much energy as he could before running the marathon.

filthy (adj.)
dirty, foul, unclean. "Your hands are so dirty. Go and wash them before you eat," said mother to Phil.

final (adj.)
last, ultimate, end, concluding. The last train to Paris is at 11 pm.

find (v.)
discover, come upon, hit upon, locate. To his surprise, Gregory came upon a gold coin in the street.

fix (v.)
repair, mend, remedy. Old Mr. Tiddles was an expert in repairing all kinds of clocks.

fly (v.)
flit, soar, hover, wing, glide. The plane took off and soared into the evening sky.

fun (n.)
enjoyment, entertainment, good time, joy, pleasure. Bethy and Sarah had a good time roasting marshmallows at the camp.

follow (v.)
chase, pursue, hunt, run after, tail, trail. Gypsy chased little Sophie all the way to the top of the hill.

fool (adj.)
silly, stupid, idiot, dinwit, nincompoop. You told her my secret! How can you be so stupid!

fool (v.)
trick, hoodwink, cheat, deceive, dupe. The sly fox hoodwinked the goat into thinking that he was a lion.

(adj.)
enjoyable, entertaining, amusing, lively. The film we saw was a very entertaining one.

Gg

gale (n.)
hurricane, blast, storm. The storm raged outside as we sat at home by the fireside.

gallop (v.)
dart, dash, race, fly, speed. The horse sped across the plains with the messenger carrying an urgent message to the king on it.

gang (n.)
band, club, mob, group, pack. The band of robbers looted people and kept the loot in a secret cave.

garbage (n.)
junk, rubbish, litter, scraps, refuse. I'm not going anywhere near that heap of rubbish. It smells awful.

gasp (v.)
pant, puff, labour for breath, choke, exclaim. Mr. Wilson panted while climbing the stairs as he was old and weak.

gate (n.)
door, entrance, exit, gateway, access. Jenny locked the door when she went out.

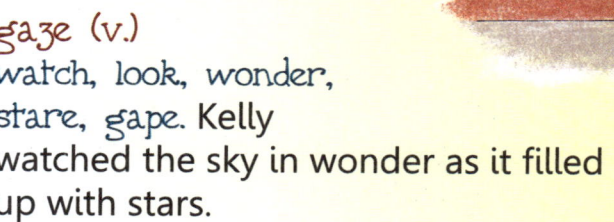

gaze (v.)
watch, look, wonder, stare, gape. Kelly watched the sky in wonder as it filled up with stars.

generous (adj.)
bighearted, liberal, unselfish. My sister is very bighearted. She shares her goodies with everyone.

gentle (adj.)
i) tender, kind, compassionate, humane, lenient, peaceful. "Your wound has healed," said the doctor to Danny removing his bandage with a tender hand.

ii) mild, soft, easy, smooth, soothing. She was standing on the balcony and the breeze softly brushed across her cheek.

get (v.)
i) receive, obtain, acquire, attain. Hurrah! I've obtained my degree at last!

ii) understand, comprehend, catch, grasp. Lindsey was speaking very fast, so I didn't understand what she said.

iii) arrive, reach, make it, come. It took the sailors one month to reach their destination.

get in (v.)
enter, arrive, come. Jane and Luke arrived just when Martin was about to cut the birthday cake.

get off (v.)
exit, leave, depart. "Please exit the plane from the doors in the front," announced the pilot.

gifted (adj.)
talented, able, inventive, intelligent. Jake is an inventive child and when he grows up, he wants to become a scientist.

give (v.)
hand, provide, supply, present. "Hand me those books," said Toby to Alice. "They look heavy."

glad (adj.)
joyful, pleased, happy, cheerful. Sheldon was pleased with his results.

glare (v.)
scowl, glower, frown. Lester scowled at Jasper when he kept on teasing him.

gleam (n.)
glimmer, glow, sparkle, shine. The windows gleamed when the bright sunlight fell upon them.

glitter (v.)
sparkle, shine, twinkle, glisten. Diana was so happy that her eyes sparkled with joy.

gloomy (adj.)
cheerless, miserable, glum, sad, blue. Wanda wept as she was miserable and unable to find her mother after school.

36

glue (v.)
stick, paste, fix, gum, seal. You must stick all the torn pieces of paper back together.

go (v.)
i) leave, exit, depart, proceed, move. If you have to leave, then leave now or else you'll be late.

ii) agree, blend, suit, fit. Does the blue blazer suit the black pant?

gorgeous (v.)
stunning, attractive, beautiful, lovely, pretty, splendid. "The flowers in your garden are so lovely," said Karine to her aunt.

grand (adj.)
magnificent, majestic, great, glorious, noble. When we went to Europe, we saw some magnificent cathedrals and castles.

grant (v.)
i) give, bestow, award, present, donate. The rich businessman gave a huge donation to the Park Street Orphanage.

ii) permit, allow, agree to, consent to. Thanks for permitting me to go out and play, Dad. I'll surely study when I come back.

grasp (v.)
catch, clutch, grip, seize, grab. Princess Fiona was delivered from the clutches of the evil curse by the heroic ogre.

green (adj.)
fresh, new, flourishing, grassy, blooming. After the first rains, the trees looked washed and new.

greet (v.)
meet, receive, welcome, hail. Amelia ran to meet uncle Albert and gave him a big hug.

grief (n.)
sorrow, sadness, heartbreak, misery, distress. Emily was full of sorrow when her cat died.

grim (adj.)
stern, severe, harsh, hard, cold. The stern headmaster checked the children's uniforms every morning.

grouchy (adj.)
sulky, sullen, moody, glum, cross, out of humour. Barry was sulky all day because his team had lost the match.

grow (v.)
i) develop, increase, expand, extend. Looks like your height has increased since the last time we measured it.

ii) breed, cultivate, nurture, raise. Grandfather cultivates fruits and vegetables in his backyard.

guard (v.)
protect, watch, defend, shield. Don't worry Peggy. I'll protect you from this ferocious dog.

guide (v.)
lead, direct, steer, pilot. "Can you please direct us to our seats?" asked Alice.

gurgle (v)
spash, ripple, babble. Timmy threw a stone into the pond and watched the water ripple.

gush (v.)
i) flood, flow, jet, rush. "This stream of water flows downhill into a cave," explained the explorer.

ii) babble, chatter, jabber. Sally did not stop babbling about the new restaurant the whole day through.

gust (n.)
breeze, blow, puff, rush. "Shut the windows, Patrick. Do you not feel the cold breeze coming in from outside?" said mother.

Hh

habit (n.)
practice, tendency, routine, custom, tradition. It was a part of Hilda's routine to feed the birds every morning.

haggle (v.)
bargain, quarrel, bicker, squabble, wrangle. Grace went to the supermarket and bargained hard for a lower price.

harden (v.)
solidify, stiffen, set, freeze. These toffees have to set before they are ready to eat.

halt (v.)
stop, pull up, cease, pause. The driver stopped the bus suddenly to avoid hitting the dog that was crossing the road.

hamper (v.)
block, prevent, hinder, obstruct, thwart. The heavy rains prevented us from doing anything useful.

handsome (adj.)
good-looking, elegant, attractive, pleasing. "Your son has grown up to be a very good-looking young man," said Aunt Betsy to Paul's mother.

handy (adj.)
convenient, practical, useful, efficient. "Now this is a very convenient peg to hook my umbrella," said Grandpa.

haphazard (adj.)
aimless, random, disorganized, chaotic, purposeless. "Why is your room so disorganized? I can't find anything!" Katie's elder sister asked her.

happen (v.)
occur, take place, come about, result. The police officer diverted the traffic to another road as an accident had taken place.

happy (adj.)
lighthearted, glad, joyful, satisfied, delighted, pleased. Robin whistled and walked lightheartedly down the forest path.

hard (adj.)
i) solid, firm, rigid, stiff. I need a firm pillow to sleep on, not a soft one.
ii) difficult, tough, complex. The sums that were given in the test were very difficult.

hardship (n.)
difficulty, suffering, burden, trouble, misfortune. It's such a beautiful day outside. This is not the time to sit and whine about all the difficulties in life.

harm (v.)
wound, injure, hurt, damage. The dog playfully bit the cat and injured it.

harsh (adj.)
rough, tough, severe. The mountain climbers found themselves in very severe conditions.

hate (v.)
dislike, detest, loathe, despise. I detest this rainy weather. When is the sun going to come out?

haughty (adj.)
proud, snobbish, arrogant, high, snooty, conceited. Nobody liked Caroline because she was snobbish and did not talk nicely to people.

have (v.)
own, possess, keep, hold, carry. Leon was proud to own a new bicycle.

havoc (n.)
devastation, destruction, desolation, waste, ruin. The flood left a lot of destruction in its wake.

head (n.)
i) brain, mind, intellect. You have to think about this problem with a calm mind, or else you'll not come up with a solution.
ii) top, peak, tip, apex. You'll find Bryan at the top of the stairs.
iii) chief, boss, leader, manager, principal, supervisor. Joshua was the leader of the school band.

(v.)
proceed, go, move, turn, steer. We proceeded towards the beach after resting.

healthy (adj.)
well, hale and hearty, sound, strong, fit. Grandpa was hale and hearty even at the age of ninety.

heap (n.)
stack, pile, mass, collection. "The book you are looking for is not in this stack," said the librarian to Tom.

heavy (adj.)
weighty, bulky, massive. Aunt Tabitha was carrying a very bulky suitcase when she landed in New York.

heed (v.)
follow, regard, notice, mind. Follow my advice and you'll do well.

help (v.)
assist, aid, support, benefit. Gerald's mother assisted him with his homework.

hero (n.)
idol, star, superstar, champion. Billy became a star in his school because he made the basketball team get the Championship trophy.

high (adj.)
tall, lofty, elevated, soaring. The eagle is a bird that can soar very high.

hilarious (adj.)
funny, amusing, humorous, jolly, entertaining. The joke was so funny, that Andy fell on the floor laughing.

hit (v.)
strike, blow, slam, beat. Grandma Brown struck the thief with her handbag.

hoard (v.)
store, collect, gather, accumulate, save. Farmer Joe collected the ripe wheat from his field and stored it in the granary.

hoarse (adj.)
raspy, rough, harsh, gruff, throaty. Hank acted like an ogre and spoke in a gruff voice to scare everyone around him.

hold (v.)
grip, grasp, clasp. Tom gripped onto his bicycle tightly as he went speeding over the rocky path.

holiday (n.)
vacation, time off, leave, break, festival, celebration. Danny went to live in an igloo during his winter holidays.

hollow (n.)
pit, crater, dent, depression, pocket, hole. Dixie hid her bone in a hole in the ground.

holy (adj.)
sacred, blessed, divine, religious, hallowed. The Bible and the Koran are religious books.

honest (adj.)
reliable, truthful, genuine, trustworthy, upright. The eyewitness's report was genuine.

hope (n.)
expect, long, look forward to, desire, anticipate. Aunt Polly scattered the seeds and looked forward to them giving rise to strong trees.

horrible (adj.)
awful, terrible, dreadful, horrid, hideous. The monster looked slimy and terrible.

hot (adj.)
boiling, burning, heated, blazing. Oh my! You're burning with fever. I'll take you to the doctor immediately.

hunt (v.)
search, quest, look, seek. Jack's search for the pirate's treasure led him into a dark cave.

hurl (v.)
fling, chuck, throw, toss, pitch. None of the boys can fling a stone as far as I can.

hurry (v.)
haste, rush, flurry. While leaving the ball in haste, Cinderella left one of her slippers behind.

Ii

identical (adj.)
same, duplicate, alike. "You have the same bag that I have," said Dora to Regina.

identify (v.)
recognize, spot, pick out, know, tell. It was difficult to recognize Joe in his Dracula disguise.

idle (adj.)
lazy, slothful, sluggish, lethargic. The warm sunshine makes me slothful and I could lie here the whole day.

ill (adj.)
unwell, sick, diseased, ailing. Holly sat on her bed all day because she was sick.

illness (n.)
disease, sickness, ailment, disorder, malady. "No matter what happens to you, in sickness and in health, I will be with you," said the husband to his wife.

imagine (v.)
create, conjure up, think up, conceive, picture, fantasize. Chelsea stood and happily pictured herself as a beauty queen.

imitate (v.)
ape, copy, mimic, reproduce, mirror. Rollo the clown could mimic animal sounds very well.

immense (adj.)
enormous, gigantic, great, large, vast. David roamed through fields and forests in his journey and at last reached an enormous castle.

impertinent (adj.)
pert, rude, unmannerly, cheeky, impolite. It is impolite to watch TV when someone's talking about something important to you.

implore (v.)
plead, pray, beg, urge. Melvin pleaded with his teacher not to give him detention.

impolite (adj.)
rude, disrespectful, ill-mannered, bad-mannered, rough, uncouth. Sally, it is rude to interrupt me while I'm talking.

important (adj.)
weighty, notable, valuable, serious, significant, urgent. I'll call you later. I have some urgent work to finish.

improve (v.)
better, enhance, refine, perfect. The decrease in cars enhanced the quality of the air in the city.

incident (n.)
event, episode, occasion, occurrence, happening. Andy narrated an episode in which he almost died and everyone listened to him with rapt attention.

incline (v.)
bend, lean, slant, tilt, slope. The earth is tilted on its axis.

include (v.)
contain, consist, involve, cover, comprise. This box contains a jeep and an action figure.

income (n.)
salary, par, earnings, wages, proceeds. It was difficult for Miranda to buy a washing machine because she earned a very low salary.

incomplete (adj.)
broken, imperfect, lacking, short, unfinished, wanting. Pearl was tense about her unfinished work.

incorrect (adj.)
wrong, mistaken, false, inaccurate, untrue. Larry was wrong about it raining today.

increase (v.)
rise, gain, multiply, enlarge, expand. "Whee!" we went, as the roller coaster gained speed.

incredible (adj.)
extraordinary, astonishing, astounding, marvellous, great. The acrobats performed some astonishing feats while we held our breaths.

indeed (adv.)
really, actually, truly, definitely, certainly. Linda would exercise for a long time everyday. She was really fit!

infant (n.)
newborn, child, tot, baby. Harry and Sally went to the room in the hospital where all the newborns were kept.

inner (adj.)
interior, internal, inner, inside. The internal organs are quite delicate.

inspect (v.)
check, scan, examine, investigate, search. Mother checked the pockets of the trousers before putting it in the washing machine.

intelligent (adj.)
brainy, smart, clever, bright, wise. Joselyn is very smart when it comes to coming up with tactics for the basketball game.

interesting (adj.)
absorbing, fascinating, engaging, appealing. The storybook was so absorbing that Macy did not notice Tim make paper planes out of the pages of her school notebook.

interfere (v.)
poke, meddle, intrude, interrupt. Ken, if you meddle with my work, you're going to be in deep trouble.

intrude (v.)
encroach, trespass, interfere, interrupt, meddle. Barney trespassed on the museum grounds even though there was a sign that said 'Keep Off'.

invalid (n.)
disabled, sick, ill, infirm, ailing, challenged. There are special facilities everywhere in the town for physically challenged people.

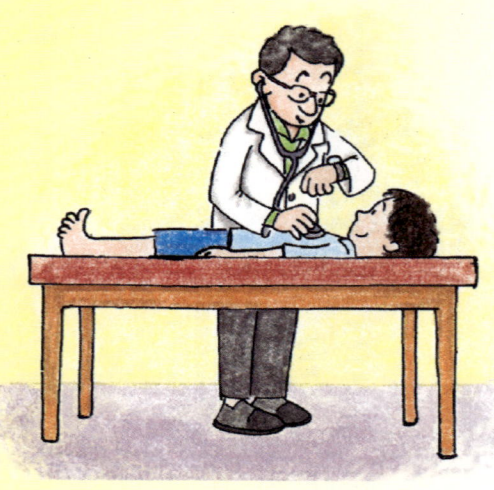

investigate (v.)
examine, look into, probe, explore, inspect. The doctor examined the patient very carefully to find out why he was ill.

invite (v.)
request, ask, call. Calvin went to call Fred for a game of ball in the park.

irregular (adj.)
uneven, jagged, unequal, crooked, rough. It was such a bumpy ride because the road was broken and irregular.

irrigate (v.)
moisten, wet, wash. Instead of just moistening the plants, Grandfather's shaky hands made him pour too much water.

irritate (v.)
bother, annoy, trouble, pester, anger. Jill tried to annoy Jack by mimicking everything he said and did.

isolated (adj.)
secluded, lonely, apart, alone. "Why are you sitting alone? Why don't you come with us and play?" said Lisa to Clive.

itch (v.)
i) prickle, tingle, tickle. Grandma removed Carl's sweater because it made him prickle all over.

ii) long, yearn, crave, hunger, desire. Ross was itching to go home from school because there was a blueberry pie waiting for him there.

Jj

jam (v.)
i) pack, squeeze, stuff, cram, press. Mandy stuffed her suitcase with so many clothes that it became difficult to close.

ii) block, clog, congest, obstruct, stop. The landslide blocked the hilly road which led to a traffic jam.

jar (n.)
jug, container, pitcher, vessel. While replenishing the container, Ellen spilled the sugar.
(v.)
rattle, shake, jolt, vibrate, disturb. The earthquake shook our house but luckily no damage was done.

jaunt (n.)
outing, excursion, stroll, trip, ramble. Pat liked to go on short trips to the beach or the hills to escape the busy city.

jerk (v.)
jolt, vibrate, shake, pull, tug, yank. Our caravan jolted along the dirt road.

jiggle (v.)
wobble, shake, wiggle. It was fun to see the jelly wobbling all over.

jingle (v.)
clink, tinkle, ring. The chimes tinkled softly in the breeze.

jittery (adj.)
fidgety, jumpy, edgy, nervous, shaky. Kimberley was nervous before going up on stage.

join (v.)
i) connect, combine, unite, link. The mother looked fondly at her daughter while she stuck out her tongue, intently connecting the dots in her new activity book.

ii) sign up, enroll, enlist. Tracy likes horse riding, so she's enrolled herself into riding school.

joke (v.)
jest, kid, tease, taunt. "But I was only kidding, please don't scold me" said Tumothy.

jolly (adj.)
gleeful, jovial, merry, mirthful. Everyone was gleeful when the New year arrived.

jot (v.)
write, note, scribble, record, mark. "I'll just write this down," said the reporter to the detective who was narrating the events of the case.

jump (v.)
leap, spring, bound, skip, hop. In the middle of the show, the lion suddenly sprang at its trainer and tried to attack him.

just (adj.)
impartial, fair, upright, unbiased, righteous. Uncle, please be fair. You gave Patty two chocolates but you gave me only one.

(adv.)
i) scarcely, barely, hardly, recently. I missed my school bus by barely a minute and so I had to walk to school.

ii) exactly, precisely, perfectly, completely, fully. "This is exactly the gift I wanted for my birthday!" exclaimed Sue, admiring her new doll house.

journey (n.)
expedition, trip, excursion, travel, voyage. Jeremy and Clara had fun riding a horse when they went on a trip to the seaside.

juice (n.)
sap, liquid, fluid, extract, essence. The sap from the rubber tree is collected to make natural rubber.

jumble (n.)
mess, disorder, muddle, tangle, confusion, mixture. This room is in such a mess that I can't even walk in it.

jut (v.)
stick out, poke, project, bulge. Laura jumped with fright when the mouse poked its head out of the mouse hole.

Kk

keepsake (n.)
token, memento, souvenir, symbol, remembrance. Steve received a memento from his class when he was leaving the school to go to another town.

keg (n.)
cask, drum, barrel, vat, container. The donkey pulled a carriage which carried barrels of oil.

key (n.)
clue, solution, explanation, answer. "How can I solve this problem then? I don't have a single clue," said Leon.

keen (adj.)
i) eager, avid, intense, zealous. Ella eagerly posed for the artist so that he could sketch her portrait.

ii) sharp, fine, acute, piercing. The blacksmith was proud of the sharp blade of the sword he had forged.

keep (v.)
i) stack, place, stow, put. Matt stowed all the old toys in the garage.

ii) have, hold, maintain, possess. "If I have this magic lamp, I'll be rich and powerful," thought the evil wizard to himself.

ii) continue, endure, persist. If it continues raining like this, we'll never make it to the station on time.

kid (v.)
i) joke, jest, tease. Harry did not like Paul teasing him so he pushed him.

(n.)
ii) child, youngster, youth. The naughty child broke the vase and ran away.

kidnap (v.)
carry off, abduct, capture, hold to ransom, steal. The robbers abducted the princess and asked the king for a ransom.

kill (v.)
murder, slay, destroy. Brave little John slew the giant with his sword.

kin (n.)
family, relative, relation. Granny framed a photograph of her favourite grandchildren in the family.

kind (adj.)
considerate, caring, compassionate, affectionate, loving. It was considerate of Nicole to help the blind man cross the road.

kindle (v.)
i) light, ignite, set fire to, set on fire. Neil ignited the fireworks and took cover. And then, boy, how they lit up the sky!

ii) excite, rouse, awaken, provoke, incite, stir up. The evil witch only intended to stir up hatred amongst the people.

king (n.)
monarch, ruler, emperor, lord. The powerful Persian monarch got rich gifts from all over the world.

kit (n.)
set, gear, equipment. Put the golf set in the boot, please.

knack (n.)
talent, skill, knack, ability. Dad is very skilled at building the most amazing tree-houses.

knock (v.)
rap, tap, beat, pound. A man, wet from the storm outside, rapped on the door for shelter.

knock down (v.)
destroy, level, demolish, smash, wreck. The steam roller levelled the rugged land so that a road could be made.

knot (v.)
tie, loop. The mountain climber tied himself tight so there was no way he could fall.

know (v.)
understand, comprehend, judge, perceive. Rory is a scientist. He understands how this robot works.

Li

label (n.)
tag, sticker, slip, ticket. The coach told all the players to put a tag on their bags so that they don't get mixed up.

lack (v.)
need, shortage, want, need, absence. The poor family was starving and was in need of food. Thankfully, we collected money and bought them a meal.

laden (adj.)
burdened, loaded, weighed down, full. Down came the tired donkey by the dusty road, burdened with goods too heavy for it to carry.

lady (n.)
woman, female, dame. "I saw a woman yesterday who wore the most beautiful dress I have ever seen!" exclaimed Sandra.

lag (v.)
linger, straggle, delay, trail, tarry. Scott lingered a while to appreciate the beauty of the sunset.

laid-back (adj.)
easy-going, relaxed, unhurried. Now that the exams were over, Matthew could finally be relaxed and carefree.

lament (v.)
grieve, mourn, sorrow, weep. The seven dwarfs mourned the death of Snow White after she bit the poisoned apple.

land (v.)
ground, soil, field, soil. The cheetah runs so fast that it covers a lot of ground every minute.

lane (n.)
path, passage, road, way. Take the path on the left and go straight to reach the mall.

51

lap (v.)
i) orbit, round, course, circle, circuit. Every morning, Julia ran five rounds of the park.

ii) lick, sip, drink. The cat licked all the milk off the saucer and then ran away.

large (adj.)
huge, big, enormous, giant, great, vast. Roger rested under the great oak tree.

lash (v.)
beat, dash, hit, pound, strike. Strong winds that hit the coast of California caused a lot of damage.

latch (v.)
lock, fasten, bolt, secure. "You better stay at home, Banjo," said Victor, bolting the gate.

laugh (v.)
guffaw, chuckle, chortle, chuckle, giggle. "I know it's bad manners, but I only dip the biscuit in my tea when I am alone," chuckled Grandpa.

lay (v.)
settle, place, leave, plant, set down. The nurse settled the new born baby in the crib.

lead (v.)
guide, direct, show, pilot, conduct. The smart dog guided the blind man to the park.

leak (v.)
ooze, trickle, seep, spill, discharge. The liquid oozed out from the hole in the side of the tube.

lean (v.)
tilt, slant, bend, incline, slope. This picture on the wall slants too much to the left. Straighten it before falls.

(adj.)
slim, thin, skinny, slender, lanky. Oliver was the only one among us who was skinny enough to slip into the garden through the narrow opening in the wall.

learn (v.)
i) master, train, acquire, grasp, pick up. "You must train yourself to concentrate on the ball," said the coach.

ii) discover, find out, understand, gather, hear. When the detective discovered the third clue, he immediately realised who the murderer was.

leave (v.)
go away, desert, abandon, exit, disappear. "You must go away from here before the witch comes again," the bird warned Harry.

lengthen (v.)
stretch, extend, continue, elongate, expand, increase. Jason stretched the rubber band to see how far it'll extend without breaking.

lecture (v.)
talk, instruct, speak, address. The principal addressed the whole school about the importance of discipline.

legible (adj.)
neat, plain, readable, clear, understandable. It is a joy to read Tina's handwriting because it is so neat.

less (adj.)
fewer, smaller, shorter, lesser, reduced. I don't want a whole essay. Write a fewer lines than what you have already written about your summer holidays.

let (v.)
allow, permit, grant. I am sorry madam, but we do not allow pet dogs at the railway station.

lethal (adj.)
deadly, mortal, fatal. Many snakes have a poison that is fatal for humans.

lid (n.)
cover, cap, top, seal. "Do remember to cover the jam jar when you are done," said mother.

lift (v.)
raise, hoist, pick, uplift. Danny raised his hands and stretched his legs while doing his exercises.

like (v.)
enjoy, love, fancy, enjoy, adore, admire. I love to go into my secret room upstairs and read.

line (n.)
i) row, file, column. Robin planted two rows of peas in his vegetable garden.

ii) mark, dash, stroke, streak. Hilda made a stroke across the page to show that all that she had written was cancelled.

listen (v.)
hear, attend, heed. When I explain something to you, I expect you to pay heed to whatever I say.

little (adj.)
tiny, small, wee, mini, minute. Thumbelina was so tiny that she could sleep in a walnut shell.

live (v.)
inhabit, reside, stay, occupy. Creatures who inhabit both water and land are called amphibians.

lively (adj.)
spirited, energetic, bouncy, active, alert. The bouncy kitten got itself entangled in the wool.

lock (v.)
bolt, fasten, secure, close. "Fasten the windows properly, there is a storm raging outside," said father.

long (adj.)
lengthy, extensive, extended, stretched. "You have to research extensively for this project," the teacher told Dick.

look (v.)
see, watch, gaze, view, observe. With his new telescope, Gary was trying to see the Great Bear.

loosen (v.)
untie, release, free, let go. As soon as Frisky was released from the leash, he dashed away.

loot (v.)
rob, steal, plunder, sack. Father was robbed of all his money on the way back home.

lose (v.)
misplace, mislay, forget, miss. Forgetful Ivan always mislaid his pens and kept borrowing them from everyone else.

loud (adj.)
booming, noisy, blaring, deafening. The giant had a booming voice that made everyone even more afraid of him.

love (v.)
adore, be affectionate, like, cherish, treasure. Mike adores his father and feels that he is the best.

lovely (adj.)
beautiful, attractive, exquisite, adorable, charming. It's unfortunate that you have to work in the office on such a beautiful day.

loyal (adj.)
faithful, trustworthy, constant, devoted. Fraser was a trustworthy employee of the company.

lucky (adj.)
fortunate, happy, favoured, blessed. You are a fortunate man to have a wife who cooks so well.

luggage (n.)
baggage, suitcases, bags, trunks, things. Uncle Willy strapped the heavy baggage on top of his small car.

lunge (v.)
leap, jab, pounce, thrust, charge. Keith leaped to catch the falling goldfish bowl.

lurk (v.)
hide, prowl, sneak, crouch, snoop. The burglar quickly sneaked past the guards into the building.

lush (adj.)
abundant, rich, luxuriant, flourishing, lavish. The luxuriant vegetation in the forest made it look even more mysterious and enchanting in the twilight.

Mm

magical (adj.)
enchanted, mesmerizing, supernatural. Thomas dreamt of an enchanted forest where a monster chased him.

magnificent (adj.)
gorgeous, grand, glorious, splendid, majestic, impressive. The poor woodcutter was awed when he entered the majestic court of the king.

magnify (v.)
enlarge, increase, expand, boost. The picture is too small for everyone to see. You have to enlarge it.

main (adj.)
chief, principal, primary, central, major. The principal idea of this book is that patience always bears fruit.

maintain (v.)
i) sustain, support, preserve, conserve, keep. The old mansion was well-preserved.
ii) continue, keep, carry on. If you keep nagging me, I'll walk out of the room.

major (adj.)
main, primary, principal, greatest. The main office of the company is in the capital.

make (v.)
i) create, prepare, produce, build, construct. Fred created a sculpture of a beautiful mermaid sitting on a rock.

ii) reach, attain, get, gain. The way they're playing, I really doubt if this team will reach the finals.

man (n.)
guy, male, fellow, chap. "Mom, the guy who takes the garbage out came in the morning," Jill called out from the kitchen.

manner (n.)
way, style, fashion, approach, method. One ordinary evening, on no particular occasion, Jessie and Mandy dressed up as vampires and started behaving in a queer way.

margin (n.)
border, edge, rim, verge, brink, limit. The eagle swooped down the edge of the cliff to catch a wild hare.

mark (n.)
blotch, stain, spot, smudge. Oh no! This raspberry ice cream will stain my T-shirt.

marvel (v.)
be amazed, wonder, gaze. The astronauts floated silently in the spaceship, amazed at the beauty of the stars and planets surrounding them.
(n.)
wonder, spectacle, sight, sensation. The Taj Mahal is one of the wonders of the world.

massive (adj.)
enormous, gigantic, colossal, immense, large. The arena that the gladiators fought in was colossal.

match (n.)
i) game, competition, meet, contest, bout. Chuck's mother did not allow him to go to watch the basketball game.
ii) competitor, equal, rival, peer. No one in this school could equal Hank in sports.
(v.)
agree, suit, harmonize, fit, blend, go with. You do look a bit funny because your blue trouser doesn't go with your green shirt.

maximum (adj.)
most, top, peak, extreme, utmost. The car sped through the road at top speed.

maybe (adv.)
perhaps, possibly. Perhaps this bus will take us home.

mean (v.)
intend, plan, aim, purpose, want, wish. I did intend to go to play earlier but unfortunately, it rained.
(adj.)
nasty, grouchy, rude, cruel. Scrooge was a nasty old miser, with a cold, cold heart.

meet (v.)
i) bump into, find, stumble upon, encounter, greet. What a surprise it is to bump into you after so many years!

ii) collect, gather, assemble. We will all assemble near the signboard at exactly 5 o'clock.

meagre (adj.)
little, slight, scarce, sparse, scanty. The poor family had only a sparse amount of food because they could not afford more.

menace (n.)
peril, danger, threat, risk, hazard. The presence of a man-eating tiger near the village posed a threat to the villagers.

mend (v.)
repair, fix, patch, stitch. Lydia stitched her torn coat with a pretty flower patch.

merry (adj.)
glad, joyful, cheerful, light-hearted, jovial, gleeful. The whole village was joyful when it finally rained.

mess (adj.)
jumble, clutter, shambles, disorder, untidiness. Oh dear, I forgot to close the window. Now everything is in shambles.

middle (n.)
centre, midpoint, core, heart. Both of you sit at the sides and let Alicia sit in the centre.

might (n.)
force, strength, energy, power. The boy shook the tree with so much force that all the fruits fell down.

mild (adj.)
gentle, soft, calm, serene, tender. The gentle manner in which Thelma rocked the cradle quietened the baby.

mind (n.)
brain, intellect, intelligence. Jessie's intelligence is so remarkable that he understands the most difficult ideas.

(v.) watch out, tend, heed, notice. Watch out for the low wooden beam at the entrance. You might hurt your head.

mischief (n.)
naughtiness, trouble, misbehaviour, pranks. Eliza was up to her usual pranks when she applied glue on the chair on which Jimmy was going to sit.

miserable (adj.)
unhappy, sad, down, wretched. Why do you look so unhappy? What happened to you?

mix (v.)
blend, mingle, merge, fuse. Sarah watched her mother blend the mango and the milk for the mango smoothie.

moan (v.)
groan, whine, wail, sob. "My dress is ruined," wailed the princess.

mock (v.)
ridicule, taunt, tease, jeer. Ben was hurt when his friends ridiculed him for being overweight.

modern (adj.)

latest, new, current, recent. Robin found the new gadgets fascinating.

moist (adj.)
damp, wet, clammy, dank. Grandfather took long to light the damp matchstick.

more (adj.)
extra, added, additional. The extra cream in the coffee made it delicious.

morning (n.)
dawn, early, sunrise, daybreak. The birds start chirping as dawn breaks.

morsel (n.)
crumb, scrap, bite, bit. I watched the squirrels scamper near the picnic hamper for crumbs.

move (v.)
i) shift, carry, bear, cart, budge. Greg found it difficult to carry his heavy school bag back home.

ii) proceed, go, transfer, migrate, shift. Amy waved at her new neighbours as they shifted into their new house.

must (v.)
should, have to, ought to, need to. Tammy should wake up early in the morning if she has to catch the school bus on time.

Nn

nab (v.)
seize, catch, grasp, snatch, lay hands on. The police finally managed to catch the clever jewel thief.

nag (v.)
annoy, pester, harass, bother, hassle. The woodcutter's wife pestered him all the time about not having enough money.

nap (v.)
sleep, snooze, siesta, doze, rest. I'm feeling so sleepy after the heavy meal that I'm going to doze off for a while.

narrate (v.)
relate, tell, unfold, describe, report. The kids related all that they did in the summer camp to their parents.

narrow (adj.)
thin, tight, confined, cramped, slender. The group had to walk in a single file on the narrow path on the mountain.

nasty (adj.)
i) foul, unpleasant, terrible, awful. The garbage dump in the outskirts of the city has a really foul smell.

ii) mean, cruel, vicious, spiteful, vile. Finally, here's a movie with an ogre who's not mean.

navigate (v.)
steer, cruise, direct, guide, pilot, sail. The captain of the ship steered it very carefully around dangerous icebergs.

near (adj.)
close, neighbouring, nearby. The house neighbouring the post office is a haunted one.

neat (adj.)
tidy, clean, orderly, straight. My sister Angela always keeps her cupboard tidy.

need (v.)
require, want, lack. Regina urgently required a needle and a thread to stitch the torn part of her dress.

neglect (v.)
ignore, overlook, forget, disregard, omit, pass over. Betty ignored whatever Reggie said because he had said some very rude things to her.

nervous (adj.)
tense, anxious, worried, fearful, fidgety, jittery, edgy. Michelle was anxious about the outcome of the volleyball match.

new (adj.)
latest, recent, modern, novel, original, current, fresh. Old Granny did not feel at home with the latest kitchen appliances in her daughter's home.

nibble (v.)
nip, peck, bite, gnaw, chew. The hungry mouse gnawed at the nuts.

nice (adj.)
pleasant, good, charming, delightful, attractive, kind. This chocolate mousse is really good. You must try it.

nimble (adj.)
quick, agile, brisk, lively, active. It's a wonder to watch the agile athletes running at the Olympics.

nod (v.)
gesture, indicate, acknowledge, bow, signal. Father gestured to Barry that he could go out and play when Barry asked him for permission.

noise (n.)
clatter, commotion, din, racket, sound. All the pieces of wood fell on the floor with a loud clatter.

nonsense (n.)
stupidity, silliness, foolishness, rubbish, gibberish. Logan is talking gibberish. I think that man has lost his balance.

normal (adj.)
typical, usual, common, ordinary, regular. Grandpa and Grandma, as usual, walk their pet dog every morning.

nosy (adj.)
meddlesome, curious, interfering, prying, snooping. Please mind your own business. Stop being meddlesome.

notice (v.)
observe, see, perceive, spot, heed. "Oh look!" said Felix when he spotted a pair of giraffes in the distance.

nourish (v.)
nurture, feed, supply, sustain, tend. If you want to nurture your talent, then you must practise everyday.

nudge (v.)
elbow, push, shove, prod, poke, bump. "Uh! Oh! Mother is there at the door and she can see you stealing the candy," said Tom, prodding his brother.

nuisance (n.)
pest, trouble, annoyance. Farmer Jones set up mousetraps in his barn to get rid of the pets.

numb (adj.)
frozen, paralyzed, unfeeling, cold, deadened. It's so cold that my fingers feel completely frozen and I can't move them at all!

numerous (adj.)
abundant, many, numberless. The headmaster was happy when he saw that many people had turned up to watch the school play.

nurse (v.)
tend, care for, nurture, treat. Fred tended to Sally when she was sick.

nutritious (adj.)
wholesome, healthy, health-giving, nourishing, strengthening. "How will you become strong if you don't eat healthy food?" asked mother as she gave Sandra some more porridge.

62

Oo

oath (n.)
vow, pledge, promise, word. All doctors have to take a pledge to care for their patients to the best of their ability.

obese (n.)
overweight, fat, heavy, podgy, stout. I think I need to start exercising. I've become overweight and my pants don't fit me anymore.

obey (v.)
follow, conform, carry out, heed, keep, serve. Follow your coach's instructions if you want to learn tennis properly.

object (n.)
thing, article, item, body. Why can't you keep your things where they belong?

(n.)
protest, oppose, refuse, complain. "I'll not go because it is a Sunday and I want to rest!" protested Kelly when I asked her to buy groceries from the market.

observe (v.)
see, watch, notice, view, look at, study, scrutinize. Stacy studied the caterpillar carefully for her nature study project.

obstacle (n.)
block, difficulty, hurdle, interference, obstruction. There were many hurdles on the road to victory, but Brett finally won.

obstinate (adj.)
stubborn, inflexible, headstrong, dogged, immovable. Little Tim was so stubborn that he refused to stop crying until his parents bought him the toy soldier he wanted.

obtain (v.)
get, acquire, achieve, gain, attain. The greedy businessman wanted to acquire a huge sum of money by cheating people.

obvious (adj.)
clear, evident, plain, transparent, visible. It was evident that the mud that was in the house was there because of Snoopy. For Pete's sake, there were paw prints all around!

occasion (n.)
i) event, time, happening, moment, occurrence, incident. The tribal chief's funeral was a very solemn event.

ii) break, opening, opportunity, chance. Johnny never lost an opportunity to share goodies with his friends.

occupation (n.)
profession, job, trade, work, employment. Wouldn't becoming the ringmaster at a circus be an exciting profession? Or a clown who does wonderful tricks?

occur (v.)
happen, take place, come about, result, develop. An interesting thing happened on the way to the market today.

odd (adj.)
strange, unusual, peculiar, weird, remarkable. Jason was a peculiar kid who always kept to himself and never spoke to anyone.

offend (v.)
displease, insult, snub, upset, wound, hurt. Charlie hurt Dora's feelings by making fun of her painting.

offer (v.)
give, extend, present, provide. "What more can I give you? I've already given everything I have," said Antony to the moneylender.

often (adv.)
regularly, frequently, again and again. I go to the museum regularly because I love the dinosaurs there.

ogre (n.)
monster, giant, monster, beast, demon. I stood face to face with the monster, him waiting to eat me, and me looking at the space between his feet to make a run for it.

ointment (n.)
cream, balm, salve. Alvin applied some antiseptic cream on his wound.

old (adj.)
aged, elderly, mature, ancient. Always offer your seat to the elderly while travelling.

omit (v.)
remove, exclude, delete, skip, leave out. Tessa skipped the first few chapters of her storybook because they were long and boring.

ooze (v.)

leak, drip, seep, trickle. The liquid leaked from the hole in the side of the tube.

opportunity (n.)
chance, moment, opening, time. This is your chance to show how well you sing. Best of luck!

open (n.)
i) unclosed, ajar, unshut, uncovered, unlocked, unfastened. The door has been left ajar and the cold wind is blowing in. Please shut it.

ii) free, airy, clear, spacious, wide. The lambs frolicked freely in the airy mountain slopes.

(v.)
i) undo, unlock, unfasten, uncork, unwrap. I had to unfasten my collar because it was so hot and stuffy.

ii) start, begin, kick off, launch. Each time, the Olympic Games begin with a great celebration.

operate (v.)
run, work, use, manage, perform, handle. How does this machine work?

order (v.)
i) arrange, adjust, align, classify, organize. Paul arranged the books neatly on the shelf.

ii) command, instruct, dictate, direct. "Please read the rules before you begin the game," instructed the captain.

ordinary (adj.)
typical, normal, usual, regular, everyday, common. I prefer using a regular toothbrush to a fancy electronic one.

origin (n.)
beginning, source, root, start, cause, birth. The beginnings of civilization came a long time after life on earth appeared.

other (adj.)
i) extra, added, more, further, additional. "Apart from this magical lamp, there are many more magical things in my bag," said the wizard to the little boy.
ii) different, opposite, alternative, dissimilar. The car is parked on the opposite side of the street.

outfit (n.)
dress, clothing, costume, garb, suit. "Now, be still," said mother, "Don't move while I stitch the frill onto your dress."

outing (n.)
jaunt, excursion, trip, expedition. We all sang songs on the bus when we went on an excursion from school.

outside (adj.)
open, outdoors, exterior, out, outward. It was a great relief to go outdoors after being ill for so long.

over (adj.)
end, finished, done, closed, completed. Marty reached school when the first class had nearly finished, so he had to wait outside.

(prep.)
above, on, on top of, upon. The plane flew over fields and forests, valleys and mountains.

overwhelm (v.)
overpower, overcome, defeat, shatter, beat. Tarzan was so strong that he fought the lion and overpowered him.

own (v.)
possess, have, hold, keep. I love collecting pens. I have at least fifty of them by now!

Pp

packed (adj.)
full, stuffed, crammed, jammed, filled. The room was so stuffed with people that I couldn't bear to sit inside.

page (n.)
paper, sheet, leaf. Albert scanned his answer sheet for errors.

pain (v.)
hurt, ache, agony, pang. I had a toothache the moment I ate the ice cream. I think I'll have to go to the dentist.

pale (adj.)
faded, colourless, sickly, white, anemic. Dan turned white with fear when the snake hissed at him.

panic (n.)
alarm, fright, fight, scare. The false alarm of a fire in the building gave everyone a fright.

pant (v.)
puff, huff, blow, gasp, heave. Billy leaned on the tree and gasped for breath after a long run across the fields.

parcel (n.)
packet, package, bundle. Martha received a packet which had a surprise gift inside.

parched (adj.)
dried up, arid, scorched, dry, waterless, shriveled. The cowboy rode through dry deserts and faraway towns to look for adventure.

pardon (v.)
forgive, excuse, release. Jeff forgave his sister for breaking his toy.

part (n.)
piece, portion, section, bit, fragment, slice. Ah! Now that the birthday cake is cut, I will give each one of you a piece from it.

partner (n.)
friend, ally, mate, colleague, accomplice. Tina and her friend Katy always did everything together at school.

pat (v.)
stroke, pet, caress. Tessa was fond of petting her horse.

patch (n.)
spot, space, area, tract, land. Paul worked day and night, farming his little tract of land.

(v.)
mend, repair, sew up, fix. I'll just try to sew up this hole with a patch of cloth. I'm sure it won't show.

patrol (v.)
police, safeguard, keep watch, inspect. The police officer kept watch over the streets to ensure safety.

pattern (n.)
design, motif, decoration. Grandma made a skirt for me which had the most wonderful floral designs.

peace (n.)
i) harmony, accord, friendship. Billy and Gene got into a fight, but thankfully they shook hands and reached an accord.

ii) calm, quiet, hush, rest, stillness. I love to escape to the calm of the woods, away from the loud city

peculiar (adj.)
odd, unusual, strange, bizarre, abnormal, weird. Rumpelstilstkin was indeed a strange name for a person to have.

peek (v.)
glance, glimpse, peer, peep, spy. Melissa glanced outside her window to see if it was still raining.

perfect (adj.)
flawless, faultless, ideal, excellent. The ice skater glided faultlessly on the ice.

perform (v.)
act, carry out, do, accomplish. "If you do well in your test tomorrow, I'll take you to the amusement park," promised mom to Billy.

peril (n.)
hazard, danger, risk, threat, menace. Ralph was in real danger when the shark came near his boat.

period (n.)
interval, duration, span, time, while. As it became winter, the sun was up for shorter durations.

permanent (adj.)
lasting, enduring, constant, unchanging, indestructible. Reading good books will have a lasting impression on Miles.

perplex (v.)
puzzle, baffle, perplex, confuse, muddle. "How this huge footprint came here is baffling! Who on earth could it be?" said Toby.

personality (n.)
nature, character, individuality, temperament, traits. Alice was of a kind nature and would often take gifts for the people at the old age home.

pick (v.)
select, choose, elect, decide upon. I wonder which dress I should choose to wear for Betty's birthday party in the evening.

picturesque (adj.)
breathtaking, scenic, attractive, striking, charming. The Walker family was charmed by the scenic beauty of the mountains and took a photograph in front of them.

pill (n.)
capsule, tablet, dose, pellet. This tablet is chewable and has a vanilla flavour. You needn't swallow it with water.

pity (n.)
kindness, compassion, mercy, sympathy. Mr. Collins had no compassion for the poor and treated them very harshly.

place (n.)
spot, area, location, point. The Foley Gardens is a great spot for a picnic.

(v.)
put, set, lay, rest. Please put the chair between the window and the dining table.

plan (v.)
arrange, organise, design, prepare, devise. I have arranged the wedding party to the best of my ability.

play (v.)
i) frolic, romp, sport. The shepherd ran after the frolicking lambs on the hillside.

ii) compete, contend, participate. All the teams competed for the prize that was to be won.

plenty (n.)
lots, abundance, heaps, quantities. You should've seen the sight! They released lots of balloons in the air at once!

point (n.)
i) end, tip, spike, apex. When we finally reached the tip of the mountain, we sat down, rested and enjoyed the beautiful view from there.

ii) purpose, aim, intention, reason, meaning. I did not get the purpose of this exercise. Can you please explain it?

ii) spot, place, position, location, site. "It takes four hours to reach from this location to the city," Jeremy said as he showed us the map.

(v.)
indicate, show, aim, direct. Can you please show us where we should sit?

polish (v.)
rub, wax, brighten, clean, shine. The priest rubbed the old candlesticks with a cloth to make them as good as new.

polite (adj.)
courteous, well-mannered, gracious, respectful. Sharon was courteous at the meeting and gave other people a chance to speak before she did.

polluted (adj.)
contaminated, poisoned, foul, adultrated. Our rivers have been contaminated by all the waste we have thrown into them. Something must be done.

praise (v.)
compliment, acclaim, applause, approval, tribute. Mary complimented her sister on the way she sang.

precious (adj.)
valuable, priceless, dear, invaluable. "This picture is priceless," thought grandmother as she looked at the photograph of herself with her grandchildren.

prepare (v.)
adjust, arrange, make ready, plan. Sammy and Jerry kept themselves busy planning out a road trip for the holidays.

problem (n.)
difficulty, issue, dilemma, trouble. The Amazon explorers experienced many difficulties in their journey.

prohibit (v.)
forbid, ban, disallow, outlaw. I forbid you to play football till the exams are over. This is the time to study.

provide (v.)
supply, give, bring, deliver, serve. "There you go, Grandpa Joe," said the milkman who always supplied the family with milk.

pull (v.)
i) tug, tow, drag, haul. As much as Anne tried to pull the dog, he tugged away and refused to leave the garden.

ii) remove, pick, pluck, take out, uproot. The gardener uprooted all the weeds from the garden.

punch (v.)
box, jab, strike, sock, hit. "You're no match for me, skinny," said Henry, raising his hands to box little Joey.

pupil (n.)
student, learner, scholar, disciple, schoolboy. "When I was a student, I always paid attention in class," said Tobias' father to him.

pure (adj.)
clear, untainted, flawless, unmixed. You feel fresh when you wake up early and breathe the clear morning air.

push (v.)
shove, thrust, move, jostle. "Don't challenge me, a Hotdog Eating Champ!" said Juliet as she shoved everyone else aside.

Qq

quack (n.)
phony, fake, fraud, impostor, charlatan. Frank Walker is not really a doctor, but an impostor who cheats people out of their money. Thank heavens, the police caught him!

quaint (adj.)
old-fashioned, charming, unusual, odd, uncommon. The lonely old writer spent his days tapping the keys of the old fashioned type writer.

quality (n.)
trait, characteristic, feature, property. "You share your father's traits," said mother to me.

quantity (n.)
amount, measure, number, volume. Butch can eat a good amount of food. He wins all food eating competitions hands down.

quarrel (v.)
argue, fight, squabble, dispute, bicker. Well, we're not going to argue as to who'll get the ice creams. You take one and I'll take one and that should make us happy.

quaver (v.)
shake, tremble, vibrate, shudder, quiver. Rachel's voice quivered with fright while reciting the poem in front of everyone.

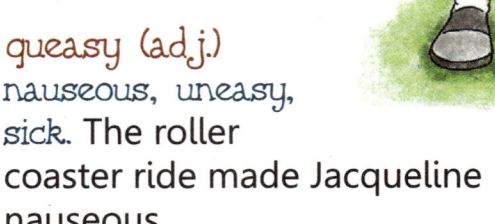

queasy (adj.)
nauseous, uneasy, sick. The roller coaster ride made Jacqueline nauseous.

queer (adj.)
uncommon, weird, strange, odd, unusual. Ah, what an uncommon hat you're wearing! Is that a pineapple I see on it?

query (n.)
inquiry, question, request, demand, interrogation. Nina went to the counter at the bus station and inquired about the timings of the bus to London.

quest (n.)
search, pursuit, hunt, journey. The detectives found it difficult to find clues in their search for the stolen diamonds.

question (v.)
ask, inquire, examine, interview, quiz. "Which train goes to Dublin?" James inquired at the ticket counter.

queue (n.)
line, file, string, chain, train. "I'll serve lunch only if you all stand in a straight line," said the cook to the boys.

quibble (v.)
argue, bicker, haggle, nitpick. Stop bickering about how long my hair should be.

quit (v.)
stop, terminate, cease, end. "Will you stop making that irritating noise or do you want me to tell mom?" said Kevin's sister to him.

quite (adv.)
rather, truly, actually, indeed. That was truly a beautiful story!

quick (adj.)
fast, swift, brisk, speedy. The racing car zoomed so fast that all I could see was a blur of colour.

quiet (adj.)
i) silent, hush, still, noiseless. Everyone became silent when the President entered the room.
ii) calm, untroubled, peaceful, serene. Jim enjoyed a peaceful weekend at the coutryside after a hectic week.

quiver (v.)
shake, shiver, quake, tremble, vibrate. Jake's voice shook when he had to explain all the mischief he had done to his Principal.

quiz (v.)
ask, examine, question, investigate. "Can you tell me the capital of Spain?" my little brother asked me.

Rr

race (n.)
contest, run, marathon, dash. You can win the marathon! So buck up.
(v.)
dash, sprint, hurry, rush. Gary sprinted to the gate when the ice cream van arrived.

radiant (adj.)
shining, bright, glowing, gleaming, glittering. As soon as Jane opened her curtains she felt the warm brightness of the gleaming sun on her face.

rage (n.)
fury, tantrum, anger, uproar. Gregory threw a tantrum when Ken told him that he had lost his frisbee.

ragged (adj.)
tattered, worn-out, shabby, unkempt, patched. The children were poor and in tattered clothes but they ran around happily.

ram (v.)
crash, slam, hit, drive. Hey, be careful! You'll crash into my vegetable cart!

ramshackle (adj.)
rickety, crumbling, broken-down, tumble-down, tottering. Doug entered the tumble-down cottage, removed the cobwebs on his way, climbed the ladder to the attic and made it his secret hiding place.

ransack (v.)
loot, pillage, sack, plunder, raid. "A gang of robbers with long moustaches arrived and looted the whole village," said the grieving grocer to the Sheriff.

rapid (adj.)
fast, swift, speedy, quick, flying. Jenny took quick steps as she was getting late for school.

rare (adj.)
scarce, uncommon, unusual, limited. Food was scarce during the war.

rattle (v.)
clatter, shake, vibrate, jiggle, jolt. We all were startled when suddenly, a plate fell down on the ground with a loud clatter.

ray (n.)
shaft, flash, bar, gleam. As he turned on the flashlight, a shaft of light lit up the toys Matthew had, making them look alive.

reap (v.)
gather, collect, bring in, garner, obtain. The farmers gathered their harvest with great joy and delight.

receive (v.)
accept, welcome, acquire, get, obtain. Hugo welcomes all the good and the bad things that happen to him with equal joy.

recover (v.)
regain, salvage, find again, get back, retrieve. The divers salvaged the sunken treasure.

refresh (v.)
revive, renew, freshen, cool, stimulate. The glass of cold water revived him after his journey through the desert.

refuge (n.)
shelter, safety, security, protection. Sam took shelter from the rain beneath a large oak tree.

region (n.)
area, zone, territory, section, sector. There are large orchards in this area that produce the best apples.

rejoice (v.)
delight, celebrate, revel, be glad, glory. Everyone celebrated when they came to know that a new baby had been born in the family.

relax (v.)
rest, calm, unwind, soothe, calm down. After a nice long afternoon at the park with his grandchildren, grandfather rested peacefully on his chair.

reliable (adj.)
trustworthy, dependable, faithful, responsible. A trustworthy person told me that there is a treasure buried near the well. But don't tell this to anyone.

relief (n.)
respite, comfort, refreshment. It was a respite from the heat when it rained.

remark (v.)
comment, mention, say, state, observe. I heard Carol mention that the weather wasn't particularly good for a stroll today.

remember (v.)
recall, recollect, recognize. Tracy tried to recollect where exactly she had kept her watch before she lost it.

remote (adj.)
isolated, secluded, distant, solitary. The explorers went to the most isolated parts of Africa.

repair (v.)
mend, fix, patch, restore, make good. "One more nail to complete mending this shoe and it'll look as good as new," said Henry.

reply (v.)
respond, answer, react, write back. William responded to all the letters he received everyday.

rescue (v.)
deliver, save, free, recover, salvage.

"Thank God!" cried the lifeguard, "I have managed to save her."

reserve (v.)
save, book, store, hold, keep. Bruce booked his tickets in advance for the movie show.

reside (v.)
inhabit, live, settle, stay, lodge, abide. I wouldn't like to live in a lonely area.

rest (v.)
i) relax, calm down, sleep, lie down, doze. There is nothing more relaxing than a nice, hot shower after a long tiring day.
ii) others, remainder, balance, leftover, residue. Call the others who are standing out in the sun too for some refreshments.

restless (adj.)
jumpy, fidgety, agitated, anxious, fretful, uneasy.  Pearl was fidgety as she was tense about little Fanny playing and breaking things at the supermarket.

result (n.)
outcome, fruit, consequence, conclusion, effect. The outcome of Puss in Boots' clever plan was that his master got married to the princess.

reveal (v.)
uncover, expose, display, disclose. The newspapers uncovered the truth about the corrupt politician.

revise (v.)
change, redo, alter, modify. The teacher told Molly to redo her assignment as it was very untidy.

rich (adj.)
i) wealthy, prosperous, affluent, well-off. In a kingdom far away, there lived a wealthy merchant who was very unhappy.
ii) fertile, abundant, fruitful, bountiful. There was abundant food in the area near the river because of the rich soil there.

rise (v.)
climb, ascend, arise, go up, soar. The balloon soared gradually into the sky.

risk (v.)
endanger, peril, hazard, venture. The people's lives were endangered while the ship was sinking, but luckily they escaped safely.

road (n.)
street, avenue, course, lane, path, route. I live in a busy street.

roam (v.)
wander, drift, stray, walk, stroll. The boys drifted all across Africa in search of adventure.

rob (v.)
steal, loot, mug, plunder, sack. The robbers looted the bank in broad daylight. But thankfully the police caught them.

rot (v.)
decay, spoil, corrupt, decompose, go bad. Carol turned up her nose in disgust when she saw the decaying food on the table.

rough (adj.)
coarse, uneven, jagged, irregular, broken. The scullery maid's hands had become coarse after years of washing dishes and scrubbing floors.

rub (v.)
scrub, massage, wipe, clean. "I have a bit of a headache. Can you please massage my head for a while?" Shirley asked her mother.

rule (n.)
order, law, guideline, principle. Any failure to obey the law of the land will lead to a penalty or imprisonment.
(v.)
govern, administer, lead, control, reign. The kingdom prospered and everyone was happy when it was governed by a wise and just ruler.

Ss

sad (adj.)
gloomy, unhappy, joyless, blue, down, low. Eva was blue all day because she did not win the first prize.

safe (adj.)
i) protected, secure, guarded, defended. You can deposit your valuables here. This locker is secure.

ii) unharmed, unhurt, uninjured, unbroken, intact. "Don't worry son, your toys will remain intact in the box," the father reassured the son when the toys were being shifted in a truck.

sale (n.)
discount, bargain. I got this shirt on discount.

save (v.)
rescue, deliver, free, help. Will you rescue my little teddy bear too, Mr. Fire Fighter?

say (v.)
speak, tell, remark, speech, utter. Can you please tell me what happened at the place of the accident?

scatter (v.)
strew, disperse, sprinkle, spread. The leaves dispersed over the ground in autumn.

scold (v.)
rebuke, reprimand, reproach, reprove. Aunt Bertha rebuked Gina for not wearing warm clothes as it was a cold day.

scream (v.)
shriek, screech, cry, yell, squeal. The evil witches laughed and screeched when they flew into the town on their brooms.

search (v.)
seek, look for, explore, investigate, sift. "I seek a princess with a pure heart," said the prince to his mother.

separate (v.)
part, divide, detach, split. Mother said, "Let's divide the pizza into four equal pieces."

set (v.)
i) install, fix, place, put, lay. Kelly placed all the groceries on the kitchen table.

ii) harden, solidify, stiffen, thicken. The concrete has to solidify before we can walk on it.

several (adj.)
many, various, different, diverse. My sister has many sets of clothes in her cupboard.

shake (v.)
rattle, jiggle, jolt, jar, shudder, tremble, totter. Terry woke up with a jolt when he heard a loud thud outside his window.

shape (n.)
form, figure, outline, pattern. Jerry could see the outline of a cat smoothly moving towards him in the dark.

(v.)
mould, form, design, model. The potter worked all day forming pots of different shapes and sizes.

sharp (adj.)
pointed, keen, jagged, cutting, spiky, thorny. Farmer Brown fenced his fields with thorny bushes to keep away the cattle.

shield (v.)
defend, screen, guard, protect. The tent protected us from the harsh rays of the sun.

shock (n.)
blow, start, upset, jolt, jar. Jay woke up with a start when he heard the loud horn blaring.

shop (n.)
store, outlet, market. There's a new outlet where you get good clothes near my house.

short (adj.)
little, tiny, small, low, wee. The little boy stood on a stool in the kitchen to get chocolates from the shelf.

shout (v.)
howl, yell, scream, bellow, roar, cry. Lisa yelled in pain when she cut her finger with a sharp knife.

shrink (v.)
shrivel, decrease, contract, wither, lessen. This plant has shrivelled without any water.

silly (adj.)
stupid, foolish, brainless, absurd, unwise. "What a foolish thing you've done to sell the cow for these beans which you thought were magical!" said Jack's mother to him.

similar (adj.)
like, close, alike, resembling. Your shoes are like mine except for the blue sides.

size (n.)
measurement, dimensions, amount, largeness, volume. "Let me take your measurement," asked the tailor.

slab (n.)
chunk, block, lump, piece, portion. Betty went to the butcher and asked for a chunk of mutton.

slide (v.)
glide, slip, slither, slip, coast. Ronald glided gracefully across the skating rink.

slow (adj.)
sluggish, plodding, gradual, prolonged. Ben walked in a very sluggish way because he was tired.

smell (adj.)
scent, odour, whiff, aroma, fragrance. Suzie's mouth started watering when she caught the scent of the food cooking in the kitchen.

(v.)
i) sniff, scent, sense, detect. Bingo sniffed the grass to see if he could trace the robber.

ii) reek, stink. "The kitchen reeks of garbage. Why don't you take it out?" said mother to Nina.

smile (v.)
beam, grin, smirk. Ian beamed when he unwrapped the new toys he received for Christmas.

solve (v.)
answer, resolve, work out, unravel, decipher. The detective finally unravelled the mystery of the missing crown jewels.

soon (adv.)
quickly, shortly, rapidly, promptly. Go get the doctor as quickly as possible. The fever is getting worse.

spin (v.)
turn, whirl, reel, rotate, twirl. The giant wheel whirled very fast and it made Lizzy dizzy.

spooky (adj.)
creepy, scary, eerie, ghostly, haunted. Don't ever go to the graveyard in the dark. It's creepy there.

squash (v.)
crush, mash, compress, pound, flatten, pulp. "I'm terribly sorry that your parcel got crushed," said the postman.

stamp (v.)
trample, stomp, mash, squash. The elephants trampled the sugarcane fields.

(n.)
mark, label, seal, symbol, emblem. The school had to put a seal on the documents to show that they were authentic.

stiff (adj.)
rigid, inflexible, hard, solid, tight. Tracy's muscles were rigid so she had to warm herself up before playing tennis.

strict (adj.)
stern, rigid, firm, harsh. Posner had a stern mother who would not allow him to play with the other kids.

subtract (v.)
remove, minus, deduct, take away. How many apples do you have remaining if you remove five from ten of them?

sudden (adj.)
unexpected, abrupt, hurried, quick, rapid, swift. Uncle Joe decided to pay an unexpected visit to his faraway relatives.

suffer (v.)
hurt, agony, ache, agonize. Timmy was hurt when Kylie was mean to him.

Tt

tactic (n.)
plan, strategy, scheme, method. Laurie and his friend met in the shed to plan the details of their secret trip.

talent (n.)
gift, capacity, ability, power, aptitude, knack. Shelley got an opportunity to present her gift of singing at the local carnival.

talk (n.)
i) chat, dialogue, discussion, conversation. Jennifer was shy but she attempted to make conversation with everyone.

ii) gossip, rumour, tales, stories, tittle-tattle. I heard some gossip about who the next captain of the cricket team would be.

(v.)
speak, say, utter, communicate, voice, converse. "I hate you!" Lucy told Gary. "Please don't speak to me anymore."

tall (adj.)
high, big, lanky, lofty, towering. A big man appeared in front of me like a mountain from nowhere!

tame (adj.)
domesticated, docile, mild, obedient. You can't find a horse as docile as Annabel and yet she is really fast.

target (n.)
goal, aim, mark, object, end. Barry's goal in life is to become an astronaut.

taste (n.)
flavour, savour, relish, smack. The blueberry cheese cake had an irresistible flavour.

tasty (adj.)
delicious, yummy, savoury, appetising. These pastries look yummy. Can I have one please?

teach (v.)
instruct, educate, lecture, coach, guide, train. "Pretty Rose was trained to be a nurse but became a glamourous supermodel."

tend (v.)
attend, look after, care for, nurse. Luke attended to the needs of his old mother without fail.

terrify (v.)
frighten, scare, horrify, shock, alarm. The birds were really scared of the ugly scarecrow.

thankful (n.)
grateful, appreciative, indebted, pleased. Fred was grateful to Mike for helping him out by loaning him money.

thaw (v.)
defrost, melt, warm, dissolve, unfreeze. The snow started to melt once the sun came out.

thick (adj.)
chunky, hefty, bulky, broad, fat. The kind-hearted butcher gave a chunky piece of meat to the stray dog everyday.

think (v.)
reflect, ponder, consider, mull over. Jake reflected on the series of unfortunate events that had taken place.

thin (adj.)
slender, lean, skinny, bony, scrawny. The animals in the farm had become lean as the winter was harsh and fodder had become scarce.

threat (n.)
danger, hazard, risk, peril, menace. The leak in the boat put the lives of the passengers in danger.

thrilling (adj.)
exciting, fascinating, sensational, stirring, stimulating. This piece of news is truly sensational. I must go home and tell Kirk about it.

throw (v.)
toss, fling, shy, hurl, pitch. Jackie dodged the ball each time it was flung at him.

tie (v.)
fasten, knot, moor, link, join, secure, loop. Grandmother knotted her scarf and headed towards the market.

tired (adj.)
exhausted, weary, drained, drooping, worn out. Ken was exhausted after he completed running one round of the field.

too (adv.)
also, besides, as well, further. Apart from being a good student, Basil was also excellent at sports.

top (n.)
tip, peak, crest, apex. Sybil waved at us from the peak of the mountain.

tour (n.)
trip, excursion, expedition, journey, outing. Not only did we see the historical sights, but we also had a lot of fun on our trip to Europe.

tourist (n.)
traveller, visitor, sightseer, voyager, holidaymaker. Morgan was a passionate traveller who had gone to most parts of the world.

tournament (n.)
contest, competition, match, game, meet. The tennis meet had the renowned players participating in it.

tow (v.)
haul, drag, lug, pull, tug. Now that little Gary can walk, he drags his favourite toy wherever he goes.

travel (v.)
journey, trip, roam, go, tour, voyage, wander. After voyaging across the sea for forty days and forty nights, the ship finally docked at the pier.

treachery (n.)
betrayal, disloyalty, treason, double-cross. "Your betrayal by deserting me when I needed you most will never be forgotten by me," said Clive to his best friend.

treasure (n.)
riches, fortune, wealth, jewels, gold. The fortune that the pirates had collected was captured by the Royal Navy.

trim (v.)
crop, prune, clip, cut, shorten. The royal gardener maintained the gardens by carefully pruning the hedges everyday.

true (adj.)

real, factual, correct, accurate,. The eyewitness gave a factual account of the whole accident.

trip (v.)
stumble, misstep. Jeanne stumbled on a large stone and fell.

(n.)
tour, journey, expedition. Major John has led many expeditions to unknown places of the world.

try (v.)
i) attempt, undertake, strive, aim. The detective attempted to catch the thief but he failed.

ii) test, prove, check, examine, experiment. This medicine has been tested on animals and is safe.

tumble (v.)
flop, fall, stumble, trip, plunge. Ginger, look out! The fish bowl is about to fall!

turn (v.)
i) spin, twist, whirl, twirl, cycle, rotate. The spokes of the bicycle wheels rotated faster and faster as Lance pedalled quicker and quicker.

ii) change, alter, become, transform. Cook the onions till they become brown.

(n.)
chance, time, try, opportunity, attempt. Robbie won the game as I missed my chance to roll the die.

Uu

ugly (adj.)
repulsive, hideous, disgusting, unattractive, horrid. Luke trembled at the sight of the hideous spider.

ultimate (adj.)
final, end, last, highest, supreme, greatest. Michael's highest goal was to win the gold medal in the race.

umpire (n.)
official, referee, judge, arbiter. The referee blew his whistle to signal the end of the game.

unable (adj.)
incapable, powerless, unfit, helpless. Shelly was incapable of jumping because she had hurt her foot.

unafraid (adj.)
fearless, courageous, dauntless, brave, confident. The brave little tailor killed seven flies in one blow.

uncertain (adj.)
doubtful, unsure, hazy, unclear, vague. Samuel was doubtful about whether he had to take a left or a right to go to David's house.

unclean (adj.)
dirty, filthy, foul, contaminated, polluted. The air in our city is so polluted that it causes a lot of breathing problems.

uncomfortable (adj.)
i) uneasy, troubled, awkward, nervous. Dora was uneasy in the dark damp cave. And there were bats too!
ii) cramped, hard, disagreeable, irritating, troublesome. Rosa longed to have a modular kitchen where she would not feel cramped up.

under (prep.)
below, beneath, underneath. Beneath the trees lay the little boy in the cool shade, dreaming.

understand (v.)
comprehend, follow, grasp, realize, get. If I teach you how to find your way out of the maze, will you comprehend it?

undo (v.)
open, loosen, untie, unfasten, open, unstrap. Untie your shoelaces and take off your shoes. Or else, they'll get spoilt.

uneasy (adj.)
anxious, uncomfortable, unsettled, disturbed, restless, nervous. Cathy was disturbed when she read about the recent robberies in the city.

uneven (adj.)
irregular, bumpy, broken, rough. The witch looked frightening because of her irregular teeth.

unfair (adj.)
unjust, biased, wrong, wrongful, prejudiced. The king was unjust because he punished the poor and let the rich go free.

unfold (v.)
undo, straighten, unfurl, unroll, unwrap. Aladdin unrolled the magic carpet and off he flew into the starlit night.

uniform (n.)
attire, costume, dress, garb, outfit, livery. A guard in a handsome attire smiled and greeted us at the hotel.

(adj.)
i) alike, similar, equal, identical. Keep books of equal size on this part of the shelf.

ii) even, smooth, regular, unbroken, unvarying. Thomas skied smoothly all the way downhill.

unite (v.)
combine, merge, join, link, unify. The enemy can be defeated only if the two countries combine their strength.

unkind (adj.)
cruel, harsh, inhuman, nasty, spiteful, unfriendly. It's cruel to mock the underprivileged.

unlock (v.)
open, unfasten, unbolt, free, release. Can somebody please open the door from the outside? I've been locked in.

unlucky (adj.)
luckless, unfortunate, cursed, hapless, wretched. It was unfortunate that when Gail reached the counter, they had run out of tickets to the show.

unreal (adj.)
imaginary, false, fictitious, false, illusory, mythical. These stories might be fictitious, but they have a real moral to them.

unsafe (adj.)
dangerous, hazardous, risky, threatening, perilous. Most of the rides in the amusement park are dangerous for kids below five years.

ii) disturb, bother, agitate, grieve, trouble. "Marcy do not bother me. Can't you see I'm busy?" scolded father.

urgent (adj.)
crucial, immediate, critical, important, pressing. I'll call you later. I have some crucial work to finish.

use (v.)
i) utilize, harness, apply, wield, work. Hogan utilized his truck to carry heavy loads.

ii) consume, exhaust, spend, waste. Suzy wasted precious water by not turning off the tap while she brushed her teeth.

upset (v)
i) upturn, topple, knock over, spill, capsize. The boat upturned in the storm but the fisherman managed to swim to the shore.

useful (adj.)
helpful, beneficial, fruitful, advantageous, effective, practical. I find the microwave oven helpful when I have to quickly heat food.

Vv

value (n.)
worth, importance, merit, significance, usefulness. Mother's Day is a day to celebrate the importance of the mother in our lives.

vanish (v.)
disappear, fade, evaporate, dissolve. Superman disappeared into the sky after saving the lady from the fire.

vary (v.)
alter, change, differ, fluctuate, shift. The weather seemed to be fluctuating and that is why we could not plan our outing.

vast (adj.)
immense, colossal, huge, boundless, great, gigantic. The spaceship flew into the immense regions of space.

vacant (adj.)
empty, uninhabited, unoccupied, unfilled, void. The burglar broke into the empty house and stole a valuable painting.

vacation (n.)
holiday, break, rest, leave. The children went to their grandma's place during their holidays.

vain (adj.)
proud, haughty, smug, arrogant, conceited. Cinderella's sisters were very haughty and looked down upon her.

very (adj.)
especially, immensely, extremely, remarkably. Old Aunt May was extremely touched when Uncle Rob gave her a special gift.

vice (n.)
fault, failing, defect. Caroline admitted that it was her fault that the accident happend.

victory (n.)
triumph, win, conquest, success. This win meant that the team became the World Cup Champions.

vomit (v.)
throw up, puke, regurgitate, barf. Greg must have eaten something stale because as soon as he stepped out, he threw up.

villain (n.)
rascal, rogue, scoundrel, brute, devil. The detective concluded that the salesman seemed well mannered but was in reality a scoundrel.

vision (n.)
sight, eyes, view, perception, seeing. The ship faded away from sight as it went further into the sea.

visit (v.)
go, drop by, call in, see. You can go to the museum or the park.

voracious (adj.)
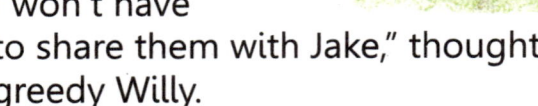
greedy, hungry, ravenous, devouring. "Let me eat these burgers fast so I won't have to share them with Jake," thought greedy Willy.

vow (v.)
promise, pledge, take an oath, affirm. Samantha promised her mother to get better grades in the next term.

voyage (v.)
cruise, journey, sail. For their holiday, the Thompsons went cruising in the Bahamas.

Ww

walk (v.)
stroll, saunter, amble, march, roam. Grandpa strolled towards the lake to spend a quiet afternoon fishing.

want (v.)
desire, wish, crave, yearn, require. The weary soldiers longed to return home since they had not seen their families in a very long time.

wardrobe (n.)
i) cupboard, closet. Betty was upset to see the jumbled up clothes in the cupboard.

ii) clothes, apparel, outfits, garment, collection of clothes. My summer wardrobe this year will mostly consist of light coloured clothes to keep me cool.

warm (v.)
heat, cook, simmer, thaw. Mother heated the tea in the kettle for so long that the tea nearly evaporated.

warn (v.)
caution, alert, inform, advise. Red Riding Hood's mother cautioned her not to talk to strangers or leave the path.

wash (v.)
clean, cleanse, rinse, bath, shower. Grace helped her father clean the car every saturday morning.

waste (v.)
squander, throw away, misuse. Pat squandered away precious time by lazing around when he could have studied for the test.

way (n.)
i) manner, method, style, approach, technique. Terry, the farmer did not believe in modern methods of farming.

ii) path, route, course, direction, trail. Take the path on the left and go straight to reach the mall.

weak (adj.)
frail, feeble, powerless, frail. Joanna became very feeble after her illness.

wear (v.)
dress, have on, don, bear, put on, clothe oneself. Uncle Joe donned a cowboy hat and looked like a hero from the wild west.

weary (adj.)
tired, exhausted, drained, spent, fatigued. Everyone got so tired in the five mile race that at the end of it, only a smaller number were left.

wet (adj.)
drenched, soaked, moist, sodden, soggy, moist, watery. It's fun to get drenched in the rain.

whole (adj.)
i) complete, full, total, undivided. You must eat the full apple.

ii) intact, sound, unbroken, undamaged, unharmed. Thankfully, we came out unharmed from the fire.

wide (adj.)
broad, spacious, vast, ample, expanded. "This bridge is not broad enough for both of us to pass," said Robin Hood to Little John when he first met him.

wild (adj.)
untamed, savage, undomesticated, uncivilized. The sound of savage animals in the forest was enough to give me a sleepless night.

winner (n.)
champ, victor, champion, conqueror. To win, a true champ gives his best.

wipe (v.)
rub, scrub, mop, cleanse, polish, swab. "Now I'll rub the sentence from the board and see if you remember what I taught," said the teacher.

wish (v.)
desire, long, yearn, aspire, want, hanker. Harold longed to go for a skiing trip.

wither (v.)
wilt, droop, dry, shrivel, shrink. The beautiful flower wilted in the hot afternoon sun.

woe (n.)
distress, misery, sorrow, unhappiness. The poor beggar was in sorrow as he was treated harshly by everyone.

work (v.)
labour, toil, exert, strive, endeavour. The workers toiled in the heat and sun to finish constructing the building on time.

world (n.)
earth, planet, globe. The mission of the Superhero League was to save the Earth from people who wanted to destroy it.

wrap (v.)
envelope, cover, enclose, sheathe. The fog enveloped the city on a wintry evening.

wrath (n.)
temper, anger, fury, rage, indignation. Aunt Rose shouted in anger at Greg when she caught him stealing apples from her garden.

wrench (v.)
yank, twist, force, pull, wrest. Dad yanked the can open.

wretched (adj.)
sad, unfortunate, forlorn, unhappy. Jack was very sad because he lost his favourite baseball.

wrong (adj.)
false, incorrect, false, untrue, erroneous. The rumour that the murderer had been caught was false.

Yy

yank (v.)
wrench, jerk, pull, tug, twist. Walter jerked open the jammed door with all his might.

yard (n.)
lawn, grounds, court, compound, enclosure. The grounds around the mansion were so huge that one could get lost in them.

yell (v.)
shout, howl, scream, screech, shriek, squeal. "I think my arm is broken," howled Peggy, after she fell from the stairs.

yield (v.)
produce, bear, bring forth, generate, give. The tree in our backyard bears the most wonderful guavas. You must try them!

young (adj.)
youthful, inexperienced, immature, juvenile, underage. Even though my grandfather is very old, he has a youthful spirit.

Zz

zeal (n.)
enthusiasm, zest, fervour, passion, devotion. Grandpa covered his ears whenever enthusiastic Aunt Harriet raised her voice to sing.

zone (n.)
area, region, sector, sphere, district. "Finally a whole area has come up where there's parking space," said dad.

zoom (v.)
flash, whiz, fly, zip, speed. Patricia whizzed through the book even before I could read a page.